The
Organic
Kitchen

Colonial kitchen range

The
Organic
Kitchen

By Lance F Reynaud & Duncan Campbell

David Bateman

DEDICATIONS

In memory of my grandmother, Catherine, who would have enjoyed this book. Give thanks to the Most High for strength!

\- Lance F Reynaud

In memory of my sister, Morag, who "always knew I had a book in me"!

\- Duncan Campbell

ACKNOWLEDGEMENTS

The authors would like to thank Damien of the Stone Oven Bakery; John and Gear of Ceres Organics; Rick of East-West Organics; Mike, Steve and Jag of Lifestream Research International; Brook of Pestbusters; the NZ Ministry of Health; Chris Wheeler of Soil & Health *magazine; Perry Spiller and Denise Pillbrow of BIO-GRO; and Meriel Watts for her book* The Poisoning of New Zealand.

Special thanks to Kay Reynaud, John Leask, Dave Fielder, Vin Redman, Max Alexander and Mary Jameson.

Thanks to Auckland Public Library Photo Collection, for photographs on page 12, 64, 130; Alexander Turnbull Library for photograph on page 34; and The Auckland Institute and Museum for photographs on the half-title page, pages 22, 176.

Published in 1996 by David Bateman Ltd, 30 Tarndale Grove, Albany, Auckland, New Zealand

Editor: Sally Dunbier
Designer: Sharon Grace
Printed in Hong Kong by Colorcraft Ltd

From the Authors

Lance F Reynaud (left) and Duncan Campbell

My grandmother was my first educator on the subject of food. She always used to say, "The food doesn't taste like it used to!", speaking from her experience in New York from the turn of the century. Her husband was a chef and they ate out frequently, in restaurants and big hotels. In those days they baked all their own bread on the premises, as well as making their own ice-cream and other desserts. Every menu was unique, and the ingredients were free of the commercial additives that dominate the flavour of mass-produced food today.

I was fascinated by the cooking utensils my grandmother brought with her when she moved to California in the 1960s. Some were unknown in domestic kitchens, and I played with them like favourite toys. Sensing my interest, she showed me how to use them and for the short time I knew her, she taught me what food should really taste like.

Before I became a professional chef, I worked on one of the enormous commercial farms that proliferate in California. This gave me firsthand experience of the dangerous chemical sprays that are used on the foods that we eat.

Then my experience in restaurants opened my eyes to the amount of artificial additives that go into dishes served to the public, and to the large amounts of pre-processed "convenience" ingredients used. Many of them are no different from what you would buy in your supermarket, yet anyone who eats in a restaurant can talk eloquently about what they charge you for one of their "special" dishes! This is why, when I finally opened my own restaurant, I decided to give people a "real" taste of food, starting with produce and ingredients free of all the synthetic chemicals used in agriculture. Then I cooked them in a natural way, part of which entails preparing them from scratch, not cutting corners with pre-processed items.

The biggest problem I faced was the lack of advice on how to prepare recipes with organic ingredients, and how to prepare ingredients that were not available in organic form. The only books which I found useful dated back to the turn of the century! This was an education in itself — learning how to bake, how to make ice-cream, how to prepare sauces you normally get from a bottle.

Because of this lack of current information, and numerous inquiries from my customers, I decided to write a book that gathered together all my experience and research, with special reference to New Zealand conditions.

Organic eaters can be omnivores, vegetarians — whatever. The important aspect of eating organically is eliminating synthetic chemicals and artificial ingredients from your diet. Along the way you will become a true connoisseur of food, and as my grandmother would have said, "I think you're going to like the taste!"

LANCE F REYNAUD

This book is all about choice — perhaps the most important choice you'll make. You can choose whether to smoke, drink or eat meat, but so much modern processed food doesn't give you the choice of whether you want to ingest artificial chemicals. We want faster food and commercial producers resort to methods that help them fill that demand.

A career in broadcasting and print journalism spanning more than 20 years only partly prepared me for the challenge of putting this book together. As Lance and I progressed, it became plain to both of us that this was more than just a cookbook — it needed certain lifestyle advice as well. There were no textbooks on the subject, so the guides to organic living you'll find here are really a first.

My task was to keep the text simple and logical, and to organise the various charts and graphs that form a substantial section of this book. It also includes an Organic Dictionary, explaining the various terms that relate to organic produce, and a guide to setting up and keeping an organic kitchen.

This book has been a true learning curve for me — I'm an enthusiastic bachelor cook who has consigned more than one experiment to the bin! But I enjoy the kitchen, and I hope the pleasure of cooking is something this book will also help you to learn, or re-learn.

Make food, not weapons.

DUNCAN CAMPBELL

Contents

The Organic Diet

"Can anyone believe it is possible to lay down such a barrage of poisons on the surface of the earth without making it unfit for all life?"

– Rachel Carson, from Silent Spring, 1962

After reading these words by this eminent biologist, the then-US President, John F Kennedy, established a commission to investigate the use of chemicals on farms. Three decades further on, the debate continues, while an estimated 25 million people are contaminated with toxic agricultural products each year.

The World Assembly of Disabled People's International heard in 1993 that exposure to these chemicals kills over 200,000 people a year, 90% of them living in Third World countries. It took thousands of years for humans to discover that lead was poisonous, and let us hope it doesn't take as long to reach the same conclusion about synthetic chemicals in our food.

In the 1960s and 70s, people became "diet-conscious", adopting various "alternative" food regimes in search of a healthier lifestyle. What most failed to realise then was that the real culprit was not the type of food they were eating, it was the poison added before they'd even purchased it. The invention of synthetic chemicals that fought the farmer's natural enemies was hailed in its day as a revolution in agriculture, but only now are we realising that putting poisons in our food is not good for us!

Just pick up a single apple. It may bear a proud label of its country of origin, but if it's been grown commercially it'll have been treated with at least two out of 23 possible herbicides, 34 pesticides and 36 fungicides currently available. In the case of pesticides, the tree could have suffered some 40 applications during a single growing season. There's no label to tell you that!

Although New Zealand heavily promotes its "clean, green" image, it should be pointed out that a large part of this image is obtained through the use of synthetic agricultural chemicals. On the basis of application per hectare, New Zealand is one of the world's largest users of these products.

Fortunately, the tide is now turning and New Zealand is poised to become a leading organic producer. Its geographical isolation means it is ideally suited to this role, since contamination that occurs in other countries can be kept out. New Zealand is already exporting top-quality organic produce, but the domestic market has been slow to develop due to low consumer demand. This means major producers tend to concentrate on the more organic-conscious export market, depriving the local market of variety and perpetuating consumer ignorance.

This book is designed as a fundamental guide to buying and preparing organic foods in New Zealand. It is not intended to replace other cookbooks; on the contrary, it will advise you on how to convert your favourite recipes, and those you discover, to organic meals.

This book is necessary because people have forgotten many traditional cooking practices employed when using foods without synthetic chemical additives and conditioners. It also explains how to rid your cooking environment of synthetic chemicals, be they pesticides or cleansers, which can also contaminate food.

There are no particular dietary preferences expressed — that is an entirely personal matter. Rather, the emphasis is on eliminating synthetic chemicals, which we consider the major culprit in today's human diet and environment.

Many types of people choose organic food for a variety of reasons. People with young families are concerned about the effects of chemicals on growing bodies, people who have developed illnesses in middle age are trying to de-toxify their systems, and older people are nostalgic for the taste of food they remember when they were young. When you cook organically, you not only re-learn traditional methods of preparation, you also rediscover food itself. From tofu to sirloin, this book covers all aspects of organic food, showing how readily available it is to the average New Zealander.

Kia ora!

LANCE F REYNAUD
DUNCAN CAMPBELL

CHAPTER ONE

The Consumer's Guide to Organics

A picnic in the Waitakere Ranges, 1908

"**S**pray-free", "Organic", "Natural", "Free-Range", "Biodynamic", "Certified Organic", "No Synthetic Additives or Chemicals" — these are just a few of the terms you'll encounter on product labels. The word "organic" is not protected under New Zealand law, and anyone can use it. This allows producers to state that their products are "Organic", or "Spray-Free" without having them tested or certified as such. If they carry no independent certfication, the price should be cheaper than their certified equivalent. The independently certified products are always preferable, but any statement of organic authenticity is better than none.

The following national and international certifications are consumers' assurance of organic authenticity. Products and produce carrying these certifications generally conform to, and in some case exceed, the standards of IFOAM (International Federation of Organic Agriculture Movements), with some local adaptations. This federation, formed in 1972, brings together scientists, farmers, processors, marketers and consumers seeking a return to an organic and sustainable pathway for farming.

When a product or farm receives one of the certifications listed, it means the product and the soil it was grown in or reared on are free of synthetic chemicals (fungicides, herbicides, pesticides, fertilisers and growth regulators). This procedure applies either to virgin soil, or soil which has been untreated over a specific period of time, eg, BIO-GRO's conversion period is a minimum of 12 months, meaning no prohibited activities (spraying, etc) can occur during that time. Even after this period, only a transitional certificate may be granted and there are further criteria to meet before full certification, which usually takes about two years.

It should also be noted that under IFOAM regulations, transitional produce cannot be exported. In the case of processed items, certification means no synthetic colour or flavour enhancers, stabilisers, emulsifiers, antioxidants, thickeners, preservatives, etc, will have been used. Strict guidelines will also have been observed in handling and processing. Livestock will have been free-ranged and reared without use of growth enhancers or regular doses of antibiotics, synthetic chemical dips or non-organic food supplements, and in accordance with certain farm management requirements.

The certifications listed are from both government and independent organisations. The list is small because we have confined ourselves to those most available in New Zealand. There are, in fact, many more independent certifying organisations worldwide whose products may reach New Zealand. In this chapter and the accompanying "Organic Dictionary", we will explain the meaning of these and many other terms associated with organic foods, to enable you to make an informed choice.

CERTIFICATIONS *(NZ)*

See Organic Dictionary

Name	Meaning
BIO-GRO	*Trademark of the NZ Biological (NZ & International) Producers & Consumers Council (NZBPC). Signifies produce organically*-grown; free of synthetic chemical fungicides, herbicides, pesticides and fertilisers in growing; free of synthetic additives, eg, stabilisers*, emulsifiers*, antioxidants*, preservatives* and colouring* in processing the food.*
Demeter (NZ & International)	*Demeter, the Greek goddess of agriculture, an internationally registered trademark. A biodynamic* approach to agriculture based on the theories of Rudolf Steiner and developed in New Zealand by the Council of Biodynamic Farming and Gardening Assn (Inc). Conforms to International Demeter Guidelines, which promote healthy growth through use of compost and preparations from mineral, plant and animal substances. No artificial or synthetic fertilisers, herbicides fungicides or pesticides used in growing. No synthetic additives used in processing.*

CERTIFICATIONS *(International)*

Name	Meaning
BFA	*Biological Farmers of Australia (Australia)*
CCOF (USA)	*California Certified Organic Farmers*
COFA (USA)	*California Organics Food Act, 1990 (State govt agency)*
NASAA (Australia)	*National Association for Sustainable Agriculture in Australia*
OCIA (USA)	*Organic Crop Improvement Assn*
OGBA (USA)	*Organic Growers & Buyers Assn*
OPC (Mexico)	*Organic Producers Certification*

ORGANIC DICTIONARY

The following brief definitions explain many of the words or terms you will encounter in relation to natural and organic products. They are not literal meanings, rather they are the explanations in the context of organics. The dictionary also identifies non-desirable elements found in commercial products.

Name	Acceptable for Organic Use	Meaning
Acidity	*Sometimes*	*The acid content of food, measured by a mathematical expression, pH. Occurs naturally, eg, vinegar, lemon and verjuice (from unripe fruit). Used as preservative, flavour retainer and enhancer. Similar to antioxidants.*
Aluminium	*No*	*Metal often used in flour conditioners, anti-caking agents and free-flowing agents. Also used to make cooking utensils.*
Anti-caking agents	*No*	*Sometimes called free-flowing agents; used in many powdered and granular foods, eg, salt, spices and flours. These substances are inorganic compounds, mainly phosphates and silicates. Often contain aluminium.*
Antioxidants	*Sometimes*	*Used as a preservative to protect fats and oils from rancidity — can come from natural sources, eg, Vitamin C, and also unnatural. Can be sourced organically, but can compromise the organic nutritional value.*
Biodegradable	*Sometimes*	*Able to be broken down by bacteria. Term is widely-used for commercial purposes and may be misleading,*

16

		eg, length of time to break down and possible pollutants resulting from this process. NB: Watch for products labelled "biodegradable" but packed in plastic — this takes much longer to break down, if at all.
Biodynamic	*Yes*	*Steiner method of farming involving interaction of soil, water, plants, humans, etc. Only organic materials used in fertilising and cultivation.*
Biological Husbandry (farming)	*Yes*	*The science of living things in agriculture. Biodynamic preparations. Use of natural elements rather than artificial chemicals.*
BIO-GRO	*Yes*	*Registered trademark of the NZ Biological Producers & Consumers Council*
Carcinogens	*No*	*Cancer-causing substances.*
Carob	*Yes*	*From the algarroba or locust-tree; a highly nutritional alternative to chocolate.*
Certified	*Yes*	*Generally used by producers as an assurance of authenticity in association with certifiers such as BIO-GRO, Demeter, etc. Sometimes used on its own by a producer to impress the buyer without any independent certification.*
Chemical-free	*Yes*	*Chemicals can be natural or synthetic, but in this context it refers to the latter.*
Cold-Pressed	*Sometimes*	*Process of extracting oil or liquid from beans, vegetables and animal byproducts, etc, without using heat, eg, by centrifugal force. Heating oil destroys nutrients, so cold-pressed oils are best used raw, eg, dressings, mayonnaise, etc. **NB:** Almost all organic oils are cold-pressed, but not all cold-pressed oils are organic.*

17

Name	Acceptable for Organic Use	Meaning
Colouring	*Sometimes*	*A substance available naturally, eg, carotene, but also chemically. Used as a food dye. Acceptable if from a natural organic source, but purpose is purely cosmetic and therefore unnecessary.*
Conditioners	*No*	*From sometimes natural but usually synthetic sources. Used in flours, dairy products, desserts, etc, to obtain cosmetically attractive texture; usually contains aluminium.*
Demeter	*Yes*	*Registered certification trademark of the Bio Dynamic Farming and Gardening Assn (NZ). Also conforms to international Demeter guidelines.*
Emulsifiers	*No*	*Modifying and conditioning agents. Used to thicken and add texture to products such as yoghurt, ice-cream, baked goods and margarine. Can be derived from natural sources (eg, lecithin — an animal byproduct) or unnatural sources; usually non-organic.*
Free-flowing agents	*No*	*Type of conditioner, used in salt and spices to prevent clumping; usually contain aluminium.*
Free-Range	*Sometimes*	*Applies to animals not caged or penned and their products, eg, eggs. Animals not kept in an unnatural, highly-stressed environment needing artificial chemical support, eg, growth hormones, antibiotics, pesticides, etc. Organically certified*

		animals and products are generally free-ranged, but Free- Range does not mean organic. (See "Organic").
Fructose	Sometimes	Natural sugar obtained from fruits. Acceptable from organic source, depending on how obtained, but still constitutes an additive.
Fungicides	No	Synthetic chemical used to control fungus. Natural alternatives available.
Herbicides	No	Synthetic chemical used to control weeds. Natural alternatives available.
Homogenisation	Yes	Process of breaking down different ingredients to make homogeneous, ie, of the same nature. Eg, breaking down fat in milk.
Hydroponic	Sometimes	The art or practice of growing plants both in water and additives. Plants raised hydroponically are usually grown indoors, and therefore should be free of synthetic pesticides, herbicides and fungicides, but only where specifically stated.
Macrobiotic	Sometimes	A Zen Buddhist dietary philosophy, originally from Japan, which emphasises the harmony promoted by eating certain foods fresh and in season. Aims to balance the Yin (acid) and the Yang (alkaline) in food. **NB:** Macrobiotic is not strictly vegetarian or organic, but recommends eating chemical-free food.
Monosodium Glutamate	No	A salt of glutamic acid, used as a taste enhancer.
Natural	Sometimes	Produced by or according to Nature. Not artificial or produced by synthetic methods; does not mean organic. Often

Name	Acceptable for Organic Use	Meaning
		used as a label to tempt buyers. Term has been superseded by the drive towards organic produce, because the label "natural" may apply only to the finished product, and not to what may have been added at source to ingredients, eg, dyes, perfumes and pesticides.
Organic	Yes	Traditional definition: Something of Nature, naturally biodegradable. Modern definition: Produce which is grown or raised and processed free of synthetic chemicals. If certified by a recognised organisation (see Certifications) it also means free of synthetic pesticides, herbicides, artificial fertilisers, animal growth hormones, chemical feeds or antibiotics, etc. Natural farming, storage and processing methods used, ie, no artificial colouring, flavouring, preservatives, etc. **NB:** There is no law which defines "organic" — this is the generally accepted definition.
Pesticides	No	Synthetic chemicals used to control pests such as insects. Natural alternatives available, eg, Pyrethrum.
Preservatives	Sometimes	Increase product shelf life. Can be derived from natural sources, eg, salt, vinegar, garlic, etc, but usually unnatural, eg, synthetic chemicals. Generally not used or accepted in organic produce, which is normally sold fresh or preserved without additives.

Pyrethrum	*No*	*Insecticide derived from the Chrysanthemum flower. Organic only from organically-grown and unsprayed flowers. Highly toxic, even from natural sources. Usually produced synthetically.*
Spray-free	*Sometimes*	*Usually means no synthetic chemical sprays used, eg, honey where hives are sited in areas free of sprays. **NB:** Does not mean organic. (Artificial fertilisers and pesticides may have been used on soil in previous conventional farming.)*
Stabilisers	*No*	*Substances that retard chemical action, eg, starches, modified starches and gelatine. Generally come from artificial and non-organic sources.*
Sucrose	*Sometimes*	*The active sweetening agent of cane sugar; organic only if organically grown and processed without synthetic chemicals.*
Synthetic	*No*	*A manufactured imitation. Additives of a natural product.*
Vegan	*Sometimes*	*A branch of vegetarianism, where no animal byproducts are eaten. Does not necessarily mean "organic".*
Vegetarian	*Sometimes*	*A diet excluding meat. **NB:** Some "vegetarians" eat eggs and/or dairy products, which are not strictly part of a vegetarian diet. Does not necessarily mean "organic".*

CHAPTER TWO

Keeping an Organic Kitchen

Scullery maid cleaning the kitchen, early 1900s

T he kitchen is the most important room in the house, because from here come all of your body's nutritional needs. If your kitchen is polluted, your food will be the same.

Insects and rodents are part of Nature's food chain and their eradication would be a catastrophe, but no matter how much pesticide you use in your home, they will find a way to get back inside. Our aim is to keep them away from your food environment and in their own.

If you are moving into a home or flat which is infested with pests, eg, cockroaches, you can assume that the former occupants did not practise good hygiene, nor were they concerned about the poisons they used in trying to control these pests. In this case you can also assume that poisons have been used indiscriminately and are still on the premises. In such situations, it may be more convenient to eliminate the infestation conventionally before you move in, then start preparing your organic kitchen.

You should allow at least two days — preferably three — before starting. Open all doors and windows and allow kitchen to air for as long as possible. Vacuum thoroughly, then clean all surfaces, starting from the ceiling down (note — pesticides do not kill all bacteria), using a disinfectant (see elsewhere in this chapter) and plenty of plain water to dilute the toxicity of any residue pesticides.

There are natural low-toxin methods of dealing with infestation commercially available, but always remember everything that kills is toxic.

Pest Control

A ll pests, whether bacteria, insects or rodents, need four things: Air, warmth, water and food. A kitchen contains all of these things and will attract all of these pests. Rubbish is your major source of contamination. Don't allow it to accumulate overnight and if possible, keep it out of the house altogether. Don't allow dirty plates to sit in the sink, or crumbs and leftovers to accumulate. Keep an eye on all warm places, eg, the hot water heater, the fridge motor, behind the stove; anywhere that heat is generated. These places should be regularly vacuumed and cleaned. Insects like living in these areas and will lay their eggs there. Check them at least once a fortnight.

NB: Cockroaches carry their eggs on their backs.

Lay mousetraps or cockroach hotels under fridges and stoves, under the sink and hot water heater, and plug obvious holes. Mice, like cockroaches, prefer living in warm places and dining out.

NB: Contrary to the stereotype, mice are not great eaters of cheese. They prefer vegetables, flour and grains.

Mice also need water, so you should not allow it to leak or collect anywhere.

There are several natural repellents available in organic form, the most popular being mint and citronella. Mint is best used in plant form, which many people grow as a condiment. Place stalks with leaves in cupboards, towards the back and near any cracks. Replace after the scent has gone. Mint repels lice, ants, flies and fleas.

Citronella is an Asian grass which yields a strong-perfumed oil. Sprinkle in cupboards and on carpets and floor surfaces to repel ants, fleas, flies and mosquitoes. The oil can also be rubbed on the skin as an insect repellent.

For rats, lice and mice, peppermint oil is a useful repellent. For cockroaches, cut the ends from a green cucumber and leave to dry out in cupboards where cockroaches may have access, replacing when completely dry.

Natural insecticides are available retail or through professional exterminators.

NB: Pyrethrum, which is flower-derived (see "Organic Dictionary", p.21), is available in both natural and synthetic forms — be sure you know which type you are buying, or try this simple recipe:

NATURAL PESTICIDE

Ingredients

1 litre of water
3-4 medium-sized whole garlics

Minimum 3 large onions
10 large chillies (any kind; optional)

Method

Boil water, chop up ingredients, add to boiling water. Boil for approximately 15 minutes, strain and put into spray bottle. Spray wherever you would use an insecticide.

This mixture also works as a repellent, and is safe for plants.

Another natural pesticide can be made by boiling equal quantities of organic rhubarb leaves and water until completely soft. Discard leaves and add the remaining liquid to clean water in a 5:1 ratio.

WARNING: *This is highly poisonous to humans and pets — if applying by spray, be careful of spray drift. Otherwise, use as you would a commercial product for killing ants, flies, fleas and cockroaches. This product can also be used in the garden, but be sure to wash any vegetables thoroughly before eating, if treated with this poison.*

Hygiene

Bacteria can only be eliminated by sterilisation, and since this is unnecessary in the domestic kitchen, your aim should be to inhibit its growth. (See "Storage", p.31.)

The commercially-available products labelled "Natural" or "Biodegradable" seldom state what happens when the product breaks down. Everything that is biodegradable becomes something else. (See "Organic Dictionary".) It doesn't just vanish into thin air. During this process, unnatural things can occur. Natural commercial disinfectants and cleansers are available. Read the labels, always know the ingredients of the product and take no claim for granted.

The most common ingredient of commercial disinfectants is alcohol. You can buy it yourself, dilute with water, then add sodium carbonate as a scouring agent and your own choice of perfume, eg, eucalyptus oil. Use this mixture to kill bacteria and germs.

Best of all is 35% Food Grade hydrogen peroxide (H_2O_2), which you buy at pharmacies and chemical outlets and which can be used as a disinfectant or for cleaning food surfaces. Dilute according to use. Eg, for a general disinfectant, 15-20 drops to 1 litre of water; for a floor cleaner, 50 ml to 3-4 litres of water. A perfume can be added (eg, natural oil) to give a pleasant smell. Food Grade 35% hydrogen peroxide (H_2O_2), unlike alcohol, is not toxic to humans and is also an excellent bacteria and germ killer.

WARNING: *Always wear gloves when handling undiluted hydrogen peroxide, as it can temporarily bleach the skin.*

Cleansers are basically abrasive scourers. There are many home-made cleansers, one of the simplest being sodium carbonate and a little water. Mix with hydrogen peroxide and use it as you would a commercial powder, liquid scourer or dishwashing liquid.

Kitchen Ecology

Having a kitchen built with only natural materials is as important as using only natural ingredients in your food. Preparation surfaces made from some synthetic materials can contaminate your food. Trees contain natural antibiotics and for this reason, wood is preferable to plastic as a surface on which to prepare food. Plastic can only be cleaned of bacteria by wiping with a disinfectant, while wood releases its own natural cleansers to fight bacteria. Wood only needs to be cleaned with hot water, while plastic often requires a bleach to make the surface appear clean.

Surfaces such as chopping boards should be made only from non-treated timber. You should have a separate cutting board for solely preparing raw meat because blood contaminates other food. There are non-toxic paints, oils and varnishes available commercially, and you should assume all old paints and varnishes are potentially toxic. Unnatural varnishes, eg, polyurethane, continue to release toxic vapours until removed. Children and pets are especially vulnerable to such vapours, and to lead-based paints. Beware of old surfaces and remove them when possible.

NB: Most modern building materials are becoming available in non-toxic form, ie, they have not been treated with toxic chemicals.

Dishcloths, paper towels and cupboard linings should be made from unbleached material, preferably from an organic source. These products are commercially available, as are organic cardboard cartons. Also available are brushes with natural bristles and wooden handles, which clean more efficiently without harming surfaces, unlike their plastic equivalents.

Gas is a more efficient energy source than electricity because it gives heat instantly, whereas electricity takes time to heat a surface. Have your gas appliances checked, especially the burners, to ensure they are not releasing excessive carbon dioxide.

Most basic cooking ingredients, from oils to herbs and spices, are available in organic form. However, such ingredients as sea salt and pepper, in their commercial forms, are assumed to be from uncontaminated sources. (Assuming, for instance, that the salt does not come from Manukau harbour!)

It is a mistake to take for granted that such items as coffee, nuts, salt and spices are free of chemicals (salt and spices may contain free-flowing agents unless stated otherwise), or to assume that a product from a Third World country will contain less chemicals for economic reasons; the reverse is often the case.

Honey is usually assumed to be "natural", but commercially-grown honey can come from hives in farming areas where bees can come into contact with synthetic chemicals. For this reason, a growing market supports spray-free honey, from areas located far from commercial farming.

Raw organic milk, from cows raised in a synthetic chemical-free environment, is available, as are organic butter and cheese. Pasteurisation is intended to kill harmful bacteria sometimes naturally present in milk, eg, listeriosis. However, it also kills the natural nutritional value, which is why commercial dairy products are often fortified. Non-pasteurised milk and cheese are available. (See Chart 8 in "How to Eat Organically All-Year-Round", p.44-46.)

Some ingredients, eg, herbs and spices, are just not available in organic form, so you may have to accept a certain non-organic ingredient where it is essential to a recipe's taste but only a small proportion of the recipe.

The type of oil used depends on whether it is being used for taste or lack of taste, for cooking, or in raw form. Cold-press oil costs more and has more nutritional value, therefore to get maximum benefit, it should be used in its raw form. Once heated, all oil loses its nutritional value. When cooking, if an organic heat-treated oil is available and is cheaper, it will be just as suitable. Choose oils depending on whether you want to taste their flavour or not, eg, olive oil in Greek or Italian dishes. A bland oil, eg, soybean or rapeseed, is necessary when making such things as mayonnaise.

Most baking ingredients are not available in organic form, eg, yeast, baking soda, baking powder, etc. However, they are available in natural form (see "Organic Dictionary"). Check their source and use your own judgment on toxicity levels. You will find in some cases that recipes baked with organic ingredients will perform differently to their commercial counterparts (see "Organic Cooking"), due to the absence of certain chemically-produced ingredients.

When buying canned organic food, ensure that the cans are lined with a non-toxic substance, eg, porcelain, to avoid contact with the aluminium can. This is because a chemical reaction can occur with the aluminium when the product is placed hot into the can prior to sealing.

Utensils and Appliances

Choose wood, glass or stainless steel for all cutting, stirring and rolling implements, and eating utensils. Cooking pots and pans should be made from stainless steel or glass.

NB: Copper-bottomed pots and pans are acceptable, providing the body is stainless steel. So-called "non-stick" surfaces may contain toxic chemicals.

Iron is second choice, but some cheap imported products are not recommended because the iron has been treated incorrectly and can flake off into the food — excessive iron in the diet can be dangerous. Aluminium is not acceptable in any cooking situation. For storage containers and eating surfaces, glass is always preferable to plastic, which can absorb or taint the flavour of food.

The following appliances are essential for utilising organic produce due to some organic goods not being available commercially in processed form.

Water Purifier

Water is your most basic cooking ingredient and it's important that your kitchen water tastes good, as well as being free of all chemicals. Any water purifier will improve the taste of your water, but for organic purposes you will require a system which removes all chemicals and impurities such as fluoride, chlorine and aluminium.

We prefer the "reverse osmosis" method because it is a three-stage process which not only eliminates bacteria but removes sediment, undissolved particles, chlorine and fluoride. It also removes the byproducts of chemical reactions and contamination in the water pipes. This leaves you with virtually pure drinking water. Similar systems are used for desalination of saltwater, especially on ships.

NB: These systems are not cheap, but you ultimately get what you pay for.

Before buying, we suggest a simple test that any retailer should be happy to conduct: Add salt or spirulina to the water and put it through the system. It should come out clear and drinkable with no aftertaste.

Do not be deceived about "needing minerals" in water; you can get all the minerals you need from food, and one glass of mineral water contains the equivalent of one year's consumption of tap water. A reverse osmosis system allows you complete control over the mineral content of your water. It also has the advantages of consuming no electricity, unlike water distillers, and having its own automatic flushing system, which cuts down the bacterial risk present in other types of water purifiers.

WARNING: *Water free of chlorine has only a limited lifespan if not stored in an airtight container. Therefore, it should be consumed within two days of being filtered because there is nothing in it to stop the growth of bacteria. The waste water from a reverse osmosis system can be recycled for watering plants or for washing. Do not drink it.*

Cooking Equipment

For stoves and ovens our first choice is always gas, for reasons already mentioned earlier, but also because it gives you better control over heat, it cooks faster and we personally believe the food tastes better.

Use electricity only when you must. Microwave ovens are not recommended because they give off dangerous radiation, which is used to cook your food. Radiation, eg, X-Rays, is known to be dangerous to humans, so we can assume it is harmful to cook our food with it. Also, in our opinion, microwaved food tastes terrible!

Preparation Equipment

Kitchen equipment is a major purchase, and you should choose something which gives you as much versatility as possible. You will need one of the items below if preparing organic food, and our first choice would be a high-speed blender, since this gives you some of the functions of a food processor, a juicer and a mixer. When making further purchases, we suggest acquiring them in the following order.

Food Processor

You will need one of these because most of the organic food items you will be purchasing are not available commercially in processed form, eg, peanut butter, humus, sauces, pureés, etc. Buy one with the widest variety of uses.

Blender

This is essential for your organic kitchen in making drinks, sauces and baking ingredients. Now available is a high-revving mixer, US and European-made, which gets better results from organic produce, such as flour and milk products, because its high-speed action introduces more air and texture into whatever is being mixed. These also have many of the functions of a food processor or masticating juicer. When choosing a blender, try to get one with a stainless steel blending container. Plastic cracks under heat and gets tainted. Glass would be the second choice, but again may be affected by heat.

Mixer

A mixer is important if you do a lot of baking or make your own desserts. Avoid buying a hand-held model — the free-standing type enables you to do other things. Always use stainless steel or glass mixing bowls if possible.

Juicer

Any standard juicers will work with oranges, lemons, grapefruit, carrots, etc. If using these juices in quantity, an electric juicer may be worthwhile. However, for making pureés, sauces and desserts, or for getting juice from, for example, tomatoes or garlic, you will need a masticating (chewing-type) machine which mashes the fibres and breaks up the cells of the vegetables and fruits. This gives you more fibre, enzymes, vitamins and minerals.

These machines are not cheap, but we consider them a healthy investment for the reasons previously stated, and also for their versatility. With a masticating juicer you can produce ice-cream, as well as other frozen desserts, make peanut butter, grind coffee or grains to make flour and cereals, grate vegetables (eg, turnips, beets, potatoes), make fruit and vegetable cocktails, and homogenise fruit and dairy products. A masticator enables you to prepare your old recipes using organic ingredients, many of which are not available in processed form. It also allows you to control your dietary intake, eg, fat, cholesterol, sodium and sugar.

Storage

Proper storage prevents spoilage, and organic produce needs special treatment. In commercial produce, some toxic chemicals are also used to delay ripening for long-distance transport, eg: bananas. Synthetic fungicides and pesticides can act like preservatives if applied before harvesting.

Organic produce, whether fresh or processed, has no synthetic chemicals, and therefore will tend to have a shorter shelf life than its chemically-treated counterpart. This is especially true of organic processed vegetable and fruit products. We have found, from personal use, that organic jams and sauces will last considerably less longer than their "natural" counterparts. The term "natural" applies only to the processing technique, not the cultivation, where synthetic chemicals will have been used. These will have artificial preserving qualities.

One of the benefits of eating organic produce is that most of it is only available fresh. The amount of preparation you give fruits and vegetables depends on whether they are being stored at room temperature or in the refrigerator or freezer. Some vegetables should not be cleaned before storage, eg, potatoes, onions, pumpkins and rice. However, vegetables to be stored in the refrigerator should normally be washed before storage. Washing at this stage is largely to remove slugs, snails and worms, etc.

When storing at room temperature, fruits and vegetables should be stored in cool, dark places, the lower the better, since heat rises. Line drawers with paper and store items in paper bags. Avoid storing in plastic outside the refrigerator, as this can cause sweating. Make cleaning easy by keeping these vegetables in one area. Vacuum and replace lining paper regularly.

As with commercially-grown vegetables, storage life varies, but remember organic vegetables, such as potatoes and onions, will start to sprout sooner because they have not been sprayed with a fungicide or herbicide to inhibit the growth. Organically-grown nuts will also go mouldy more quickly if kept in a place which is too warm or damp. Some of these moulds, eg, peanut mould, are toxic. Pests such as flies and fruit flies are likely to be more attracted to organic produce because it is fresher and free of pesticides. To avoid this problem, the storage area should be sealed to allow air in but keep the pests out. Eliminate gaps where gnats, flies and cockroaches can get in. Wash organic produce thoroughly and examine closely for any insect pests before cooking.

Grains should be stored in the same way. Organic processed foods, such as breads and biscuits, generally have a shorter shelf life than their commercial counterparts.

Dried herbs are best kept in dark glass, airtight containers because their main enemies are light and oxygen. Avoid using tins because they rust and can taint the herbs. Store in a cool, dry place. Loss of potency is inevitable, so do not keep dried herbs for more than a year. For more information, see the section on preserving herbs, p.56, in "How To Eat Organically All-Year-Round".

Refrigeration

The temperature inside your refrigerator varies from top to bottom. The bottom part of the refrigerator storage area is always colder, the top section slightly warmer and the door shelves the warmest.

NB: If you have a separate vegetable storage bin in the bottom, you will find this is also one of the warmer parts of the fridge because it is usually separated from the actual refrigerating unit. Vegetable storage bins can be a bacteria risk because they tend to collect condensation.

Always store raw meat at the bottom of the refrigerator because it's coolest, and so it can't drip blood onto and contaminate other foods. Cool cooked foods as fast as possible if you're preparing to store them for longer than a day. Put hot foods in shallow containers to promote rapid cooling. All cooked and processed foods, including butter and cheese, should be kept above raw items.

NB: Butter conditioners can allow germs to grow because of their higher temperature, the sole purpose of which is to keep butter soft. If using a conditioner, cut only a serving portion of butter to keep there, and store the rest in the cold part of the fridge. You should also remember that organic butter will deteriorate faster in a conditioner than ordinary butter, and should be kept chilled until ready for use.

If your refrigerator does not have a fruit and vegetable compartment, store these items at or near the top, especially if they are to be eaten raw. Eggs should be kept in the cooler part of the refrigerator, rather than in the specially-designed holders found in the doors of some brands. We believe the temperature here is too warm for safe storage of eggs. Cold-press oils and organic grain flours will last longer and retain nutritional value if refrigerated because they lack chemical additives, such as emulsifiers and antioxidants.

NB: Non-toxic cling-film and plastic bags are available, but we prefer paper or cardboard storage containers rather than plastic, even in the refrigerator. This is because plastic tends to sweat and paper allows for breathing. However, you may wish to transfer some items to plastic bags if intending to keep them longer.

The refrigerator temperature should never exceed 4°C. Bacteria will grow and multiply significantly between 4° and 60°C — this is the "Danger Zone". (See "Organic Cooking").

NB: While many of the recipes in this book have a specific "fridge life", it must be noted that refrigeration is just a temporary safe storage and does not destroy germs. Food still goes "off" in the refrigerator.

As mentioned before, vegetables should be at least partly washed before refrigeration. When washing vegetables, take extra care with leafy and bulky vegetables, such as lettuce, cauliflower and broccoli. Dry such vegetables thoroughly before storage because water will also speed decay. Proper washing and drying will increase storage life. Do not cut or separate vegetables until ready for use.

Freezing

Frozen foods may contain bacteria, but as long as these foods are stored correctly at temperatures below -18°C, the bacteria will not be able to multiply rapidly. Freezer life is not indefinite. The food continues its deterioration and bacteria still grow, only at a much slower rate. In most cases, frozen food should be used within six months of freezing. Thaw frozen foods in the refrigerator, not at room temperature. Once they are thawed, frozen foods must be regarded as "At Risk". Do not re-freeze thawed food. To prepare food for freezing, see the section on freezing, p.57-63, in "How To Eat Organically All-Year-Round".

CHAPTER THREE

How To Eat Organically All-Year-Round

The cook, the camp and the cabbage – Wairarapa c.1890s

Living and eating organically requires a little forward planning, so you can enjoy food free of synthetic chemicals all-year-round. The following charts should enable you to find the necessary raw and processed ingredients, for use in your favourite recipes as well as those in this book.

The charts show when various products are available according to type and variety. They contain all the organic produce and vegetables available in New Zealand at the time of writing. We have listed products commonly available in the main centres of New Zealand — the organic market is a fluid one and purchasers will doubtless encounter other items when shopping.

NB: Some products listed as being available only in certain months may be found outside their designated season through cold storage (eg, apples, pumpkins, potatoes, onions), hothouses (eg, tomatoes, cucumbers), or in general storage, (eg, nuts and flours). Buying these products out of season will naturally be more expensive. For bottling and preserving, produce should be purchased at the height of the season.

KEY

❖ Denotes month of availability for Charts One and Two.

NB: Chart covers entire season. Availability will vary according to time of season, whether high or low. ❖ Denotes year-round availability on Charts Three to Eight. In Chart Nine, all meat produce is available year-round. The meats listed are Organic (certified by BIO GRO or Demeter) or Free-Range. For further information, refer to the "The Consumer's Guide To Organics".

+ Denotes that classification applies to all varieties, eg, apples (Granny Smith, Golden Delicious, Braeburn, etc).

^ Denotes possible temporary interruptions to supply, due to importing problems, seasonal fluctuations and weather conditions.

CHART ONE
Seasonal Availability

✤ Denotes month of availability
+ Denotes all varieties
^ Denotes possible temporary interruptions to supply

VEGETABLES	J	F	M	A	M	J	J	A	S	O	N	D
Artichokes +									✤	✤	✤	
Asparagus									✤	✤	✤	✤
Beans+	✤	✤	✤									
Beetroot	✤	✤	✤	✤	✤	✤	✤	✤	✤	✤	✤	✤
Broad Beans										✤	✤	✤
Broccoli^	✤				✤	✤	✤	✤	✤	✤	✤	✤
Brussels Sprouts			✤	✤	✤	✤	✤	✤	✤			
Cabbage+	✤	✤	✤	✤	✤	✤	✤	✤	✤	✤	✤	✤
Carrots^	✤	✤	✤	✤	✤	✤	✤	✤	✤	✤	✤	✤
Cauliflower^	✤	✤				✤	✤	✤	✤	✤	✤	✤
Capsicum+	✤	✤	✤	✤	✤	✤						
Celery^							✤	✤	✤	✤	✤	✤
Chillies+			✤	✤	✤	✤	✤					
Courgettes (Zucchini)	✤	✤					✤	✤	✤	✤	✤	✤
Cucumbers+	✤	✤	✤	✤	✤	✤					✤	✤
Eggplant (Aubergine)	✤	✤	✤	✤	✤	✤					✤	✤
Fennel	✤	✤	✤	✤	✤							
Garlic	✤	✤	✤	✤	✤	✤					✤	✤

VEGETABLES	J	F	M	A	M	J	J	A	S	O	N	D
Ginger	❖	❖	❖	❖	❖	❖	❖	❖	❖	❖	❖	❖
Kumara			❖	❖	❖	❖	❖	❖	❖	❖		
Leeks			❖	❖	❖	❖	❖	❖	❖	❖	❖	
Lettuce+^	❖	❖	❖	❖	❖	❖		❖	❖	❖	❖	❖
Marrow	❖	❖	❖	❖				❖	❖	❖	❖	❖
Mushrooms+^	❖	❖	❖	❖	❖	❖	❖	❖	❖	❖	❖	❖
Onions+	❖	❖	❖	❖	❖							❖
Parsley	❖	❖	❖	❖	❖	❖	❖	❖	❖	❖	❖	❖
Parsnips	❖	❖	❖	❖	❖	❖	❖	❖	❖	❖	❖	❖
Peas+	❖	❖	❖									❖
Potatoes+	❖	❖	❖	❖	❖	❖	❖	❖	❖	❖	❖	❖
Pumpkin+^		❖	❖	❖	❖	❖	❖	❖	❖	❖		
Radish+	❖	❖	❖	❖				❖	❖	❖	❖	❖
Rhubarb						❖	❖	❖	❖	❖	❖	❖
Scallopini	❖	❖	❖	❖							❖	❖
Silverbeet^	❖	❖	❖	❖	❖	❖	❖	❖	❖	❖	❖	❖
Spinach	❖	❖	❖	❖	❖	❖			❖	❖	❖	❖
Spring Onions^	❖	❖	❖	❖	❖		❖	❖	❖	❖	❖	❖
Squash	❖	❖	❖	❖	❖	❖	❖	❖	❖	❖		
Swede			❖	❖	❖	❖	❖	❖	❖	❖		
Sweetcorn	❖	❖	❖	❖								
Tomatoes	❖	❖	❖	❖	❖	❖	❖				❖	❖
Turnips						❖	❖	❖	❖	❖		
Watercress					❖	❖	❖	❖	❖	❖	❖	❖
Whitloof						❖	❖	❖	❖	❖		
Yam					❖	❖	❖	❖	❖	❖	❖	

CHART TWO
Seasonal Availability

❧ Denotes month of availability
+ Denotes all varieties
^ Denotes possible temporary interruptions to supply

FRUIT & NUTS	J	F	M	A	M	J	J	A	S	O	N	D
Almonds						❧	❧	❧	❧	❧		
Apples+	❧	❧	❧	❧								❧
Apricots	❧	❧										
Avocados+^	❧	❧	❧	❧	❧	❧	❧	❧	❧	❧	❧	❧
Babaco	❧	❧	❧	❧							❧	❧
Bananas^		❧	❧									
Blackberries Boysenberries Blueberries	❧	❧	❧								❧	❧
Cherries	❧											❧
Chestnuts			❧	❧								
Figs	❧	❧	❧	❧	❧	❧						❧
Feijoas			❧	❧	❧	❧	❧					
Grapes+			❧	❧	❧							
Grapefruit+							❧	❧	❧	❧	❧	
Hazelnuts			❧	❧								
Kiwano		❧	❧	❧	❧	❧						
Kiwifruit	❧	❧	❧	❧							❧	❧
Lemons	❧	❧	❧	❧	❧	❧	❧	❧	❧	❧	❧	❧
Limes					❧	❧	❧	❧	❧	❧		
Macadamia Nuts				❧	❧	❧	❧	❧	❧	❧		

FRUIT & NUTS	J	F	M	A	M	J	J	A	S	O	N	D
Mandarins^	✿	✿	✿	✿	✿	✿	✿	✿	✿	✿	✿	✿
Mangos	✿	✿									✿	✿
Melons+	✿	✿	✿	✿								
Nashi		✿	✿	✿	✿	✿						
Nectarines	✿	✿	✿									
Oranges+	✿	✿	✿	✿	✿	✿	✿	✿	✿	✿	✿	✿
Passionfruit	✿	✿	✿	✿								
Pawpaw	✿	✿	✿									✿
Pecans			✿									
Persimmons					✿	✿	✿	✿				
Pepino	✿	✿	✿	✿	✿	✿	✿					
Peaches+	✿	✿									✿	✿
Pears+		✿	✿	✿	✿	✿	✿	✿	✿			
Pineapple	✿	✿	✿							✿	✿	✿
Plums	✿	✿	✿								✿	✿
Raspberries	✿										✿	✿
Strawberries	✿	✿									✿	✿
Tamarillo				✿	✿	✿	✿	✿	✿			
Tangelos	✿	✿	✿						✿	✿	✿	✿
Uglifruit								✿	✿	✿	✿	✿
Walnuts				✿	✿	✿	✿	✿	✿			
Watermelon	✿	✿	✿	✿	✿							

39

CHART THREE
Product Availability: Grains

♣ Denotes available all-year-round
+ Denotes all varieties
^ Denotes possible temporary interruptions to supply

Type	Availability	Origin
Amaranth	♣	NZ
Barley+	♣	NZ
Buckwheat	^	NZ (Sth Is)
Millet+	♣	Aust, USA
Oats	♣	NZ
Rice (all grains)	♣	Aust
Rice (Basmati)	♣	Aust, NZ
Rice (white)	♣	Aust
Rye	♣	NZ
Triticale	♣	NZ
Wheat+	♣	NZ, Aust

CHART FOUR
Product Availability: Flours

Type	Availability	Origin
Amaranth	♣	NZ
Barley	♣	NZ
Bran	♣	NZ (Sth Is)
Buckwheat	^	NZ (Sth Is)

Type	Availability	Origin
Chickpea (Garbanzo)	❖	Aust
Cornflour+	❖	USA, Aust
Millet	❖	USA, Aust
Oats+	❖	NZ
Peaflour+	❖	NZ, Aust
Rice flour+	❖	Aust
Rye+	❖	NZ
Semolina	^	NZ (Sth Is)
Soy	❖	Aust
Triticale+	❖	NZ
Wheat+ (White & brown)	❖	NZ, Aust
White wheat	❖	NZ

CHART FIVE
Product Availability: Beans & Peas

Type	Availability	Origin
Adzuki	❖	USA
Chickpeas (Garbanzo)	❖	Aust
Lentils+	❖	NZ
Mung beans	❖	Aust
Navy beans	❖	Aust
Peas+	❖	NZ, Aust
Pink beans	❖	NZ
Pinto beans	^	USA
Red kidney beans	❖	NZ, USA

CHART SIX
Product Availability: Nuts, Seeds & Dried Fruits

Type	Availability	Origin
Alfalfa seeds	❖	NZ
Almonds	^	USA, Aust
Apricots	❖	USA
Bananas	❖	Aust, NZ
Currants	❖	Aust
Dates	❖	USA
Figs+	❖	USA
Hazelnuts	^	USA, NZ (Nth Is)
Linseed	❖	NZ
Macadamia	^	USA
Muscatels	❖	Aust
Peaches	❖	USA
Pears	❖	USA
Pistachios (roasted)	❖	USA
Prunes	❖	Aust
Raisins	❖	USA
Sesame seeds+	❖	Mexico
Sultanas	❖	Aust
Sunflower seeds	❖	Aust
Walnuts	^	USA

CHART SEVEN
Product Availability: Liquids

Type	Availability	Origin
Apple cider vinegar	❖	NZ
Brown rice vinegar	❖	Japan
Canola (rapeseed)+	❖	Aust
Corn oil	^	USA
Flax seed oil	❖	NZ
Olive oil+	❖	Aust
Safflower oil	❖	Aust
Sesame seed oil+	❖	USA, Japan
Shoyu	❖	Japan
Soy bean oil	^	USA
Sunflower seed oil	❖	Aust
Tamari+	❖	Japan
Ume Vinegar	❖	Japan

CHART EIGHT
Product Availability: Processed Foods & Beverages

Type	Availability	Origin
Apple butter+	❧	NZ
Apple & blackberry jam	❧	NZ
Apple & strawberry jam	❧	NZ
Apple juice	❧	NZ
Apple & grapefruit juice	❧	NZ
Apple & orange juice	❧	NZ
Baby food+	❧	NZ, USA
Baked goods+	❧	NZ
Beer	❧	NZ (Sth Is)
Blueberry jam	❧	NZ
Bouillon (stock) cubes+	❧	NZ, USA, Europe
Breakfast cereals+	❧	NZ, USA, Aust
Butter	❧	NZ (Nth Is)
Cheese+	^	NZ
Chocolate	❧	Bolivia/USA
Cocoa powder	❧	USA
Coffee (ground & beans)	❧	Mexico, PNG
Corn chips+	❧	USA
Cottage cheese	❧	NZ (Nth Is)
Cream	❧	NZ (Nth Is)
Grape juice+	❧	NZ, Aust
Grapefruit juice	❧	NZ
Hazel malt	❧	NZ

Honey+	❖	NZ
Ice-cream+	❖	NZ (Nth Is)
Macadamia nut spread	❖	Aust
Malt	❖	NZ, Aust
Malt coffee+	❖	NZ
Maple syrup	❖	Canada, USA
Milk (goat)	❖	NZ
Milk (pasteurised)	❖	NZ
Milk (raw)	❖	NZ (Nth Is)
Miso+	❖	Japan
Mustard	^	USA
Noodles+	❖	Japan
Olives+	❖	Aust
Orange juice	❖	NZ
Pasta+	❖	NZ, Aust
Pear juice	❖	Aust
Pickled plums	❖	Japan
Pickles+	❖	NZ
Quark	❖	NZ
Rice cakes	❖	Aust
Rice syrup (sweetener)	❖	Aust
Sesame seed butter	❖	NZ
Sour cream	❖	NZ
Soy Drinks+	❖	NZ, Japan
Strawberry jam	❖	NZ
Tahini	❖	Mexico

CHART EIGHT (Continued)

Type	Availability	Origin
Tea (Ceylon)	❖	Aust
Tea (herbal)		
Camomile	❖	NZ, USA
Lemon balm	❖	NZ, USA
Lemon grass	❖	NZ, USA
Lemon verbena	❖	USA
Peppermint	❖	NZ, USA
Red clover	❖	NZ, USA
Rose hip	❖	NZ, USA
Spearmint	❖	NZ, USA
Tofu	❖	NZ (Nth Is)
Tofu products	❖	NZ (Nth Is)
Tomato products+	❖	NZ, USA
Tomato sauce	^	NZ, USA
Ume paste	❖	Japan
Vanilla extract	❖	Tahiti
Wine+	❖	NZ, Aust, USA
Yoghurt (acidophilus)	❖	NZ
Yoghurt (Bulgarian)	❖	NZ (Nth Is)
Yoghurt cheese (Lebanese)	❖	NZ (Nth Is)

CHART NINE
Product Availability: Meat

The following meats from animals reared in an organic environment are available in New Zealand all-year-round.

Refer to "Organic Dictionary"

Type	Remarks
Beef	All cuts available
Chicken	Available as Free-Range* and Organic* All sizes, whole or assorted pieces
Cured meats	Not available at time of print, but will be in the future (salami, etc)
Goat	All cuts
Lamb	All cuts available
Pork	Available as Free-Range* and Organic* All cuts, plus bacon
Sausages	All meats and varieties
Turkey	Whole bird
Venison	All cuts

EGGS	Available Free-Range* and Organic*

Bottling and Preserving

Because of the seasonal nature of organic produce, you will find it necessary to bottle, preserve, freeze and, in some cases, pickle your ingredients. It is not our intention to give complete instructions in preserving, but to provide a basic guide in the context of organic cooking.

Always wash produce before bottling or cooking, whether organic or not, to remove dirt and insect faeces, which harbour bacteria. This is especially important when bottling, as bacteria trapped will go dormant and grow again when jar is unsealed. Note that with some bottling recipes, the acidity levels (see "Organic Dictionary") are important to limit the risks of bacteria, eg, mayonnaise, tomato-based sauces and pickled products. Vinegar and citric acids, such as lemon, are used in most recipes for this reason.

Mayonnaise and tomato sauce are two major food poisoners, which is why you should closely follow the acidity levels stated in the recipes. Food poisoning bacteria do not like acidity.

NB: Many fresh fruits and vegetables are slightly acidic. Some procedures for bottling vegetables call for overnight marination in a salt, vinegar or sugar solution. But because organic sugar is not available in New Zealand, it can either be preferably eliminated or your preferred sweetener, eg, honey, used as a substitute. Some prefer to use no sweetener at all, and to use only water and the natural juice from the vegetables when bottling.
(See example next page).

BOTTLING TOMATOES IN THEIR OWN JUICE

Prep time: 40 minutes

Cooking time: 20 minutes, (For tomatoes & sterilisation)

Utensils: Stainless steel pot (size according to quantity of tomatoes)

Glass sealing jars, lids and seals

Large stainless steel pot for sterilising jars (not necessary if using oven method — see below)

Small paring knife

Large ladle

Ingredients

Whole fresh ripe tomatoes   *Purified water*

Method

Bring water to boil in stainless steel pot. Cut out core of tomato, leaving it whole, and place tomatoes in boiling water. Leave in boiling water just long enough for skin to separate from flesh and peel easily (use a fork to check). Drain off water and remove tomatoes.

Start sterilising jars. The oven method is more convenient: place jars in cold oven and heat to 200°C. Leave for 10 minutes.

While this is taking place, remove skin from tomatoes. (Wear rubber gloves for this). Hold tomato, cored side downwards, and squeeze until flesh and juice separate from skin. Squeeze into pot.

Then heat tomatoes and juice to boiling point, remove sterilised jars from oven, pour tomatoes and juice into jars, right to the top, seal jars and screw down lids very tightly.

Let sit overnight and check seals by pressing on the lid.

Organic & Dietary Tips

Sugar and salt-free.

Fruits are not usually subjected to a brining process. An easy method to use is to place fruit cut (and peeled if necessary) in hot, sterilised jars and cover with hot liquid. Other methods are to simmer in hot water (see example over page), or to simmer in a vinegar, spice, honey and water mixture and place in jars.

BOTTLING APPLES

Prep time: 25 minutes
Cooking time: 15 minutes (includes sterilisation)
Utensils: Large stainless steel pot, preserving jars, lids and seals, ladle, strainer

Ingredients

Whole fresh ripe apples   *Purified water*
Organic unsweetened apple
juice (optional)

Method

Peel and cut apples to desired size. Place in water and bring to boil. Meanwhile, sterilise jars by oven method. (See previous page.)

Once apples are boiling, pour through strainer, retaining hot liquid, and place immediately in sterilised jars. Ladle hot liquid over apples, seal and let sit overnight before checking seals by pressing on the lid.

Cook's Tips

To give apples a sweeter taste use the above method, but use two-thirds apple juice to one-third water. This method can also be used for pears and peaches, and gives you fruit with that sweet "commercial" taste, but without sugar.

Organic & Dietary Tips

Sugar and salt-free.

BOTTLING and PRESERVING FRUITS & VEGETABLES

Name	Preparation	Quantity	Yield
Apples	(See p.50)	6 medium	3 cups chopped
Apricots	Place in boiling water until skin loosens, peel and halve	8-14 medium	3 cups whole or 2 cups halved
Artichokes	Remove hard tip and dry outside leaves, trim base flat, snip off tips of remaining leaves		Varies depending on size
Asparagus	Remove scales and ends, cut to fit in jar		Varies depending on size
Beans (all varieties)	Broad beans: remove and discard pods. All others: trim ends, string if necessary and slice to desired size	450 g	2 2/3 -3 cups
Beetroot	Leave 50 mm of stem and tap root, boil until skin loosens, remove stem and root, slice or leave whole	4-6 medium	3 1/2 cups
Blackberries Boysenberries Blueberries Raspberries	Wash, inspect and remove caps and stems	450 g	2 2/3 cups
Broccoli	Trim stems, slice to desired size	1 bunch chopped	4 - 4 1/2 cups

BOTTLING AND PRESERVING
FRUITS & VEGETABLES *(continued)*

Name	Preparation	Quantity	Yield
Brussels Sprouts	*Trim base, remove blemished leaves*	*15-20*	*3 1/2 cups*
Capsicums	*Halve, stem and seed, cut in strips*	*4 large*	*2 cups trimmed*
Cabbage	*Discard blemished leaves, halve and shred*	*1 head*	*7-8 cups or 3 cups cooked*
Carrots	*Scrub and peel, cut in desired shape*	*4 large*	*2 3/4 cups*
Cauliflower	*Remove leaves, cut at stem, leaving flowerets whole*	*1 head*	*4 cups florets*
Celery	*Separate stalks, trim leaves and ends, cut in desired lengths*	*8-12 stalks*	*4 cups, diced*
Cherries	*Stem and remove stones – prick unstoned cherries to prevent bursting*	*450 g*	*3 cups or 2 1/4 stoned*
Courgettes (Zucchini)	*Clean, do not peel, use whole or sliced*	*3 medium*	*2 1/4 cups sliced*
Cucumbers	*Do not peel, use whole or slice into chips or long strips*	*2 large*	*2 cups sliced*

Figs	Do not stem	12-18 medium	2 1/2-3 cups chopped
Grapes	Eliminate soft grapes and gently stem	450 g	2 1/3 cups
Grapefruit	Peel like an apple, cut deep to remove white membrane, separate into segments	1 large	10-12 segments or 1 3/4 cups broken
Mangos	Peel, cut slices away from hard centre	2-4	2 cups sliced
Melons	Slice off ends, halve, peel and cut into small wedges		Varies depending on size
Mushrooms	Clean, trim ends, leave whole or cut	450 g	2 1/2 cups whole or 1 1/2 sliced
Nectarines	Place in boiling water until skin loosens, peel, halve and stone	3-5 medium	2 cups sliced
Onions	Remove outer and loose skin, halve or slice; small size preferred if whole	3 large	2 1/2 cups chopped
Parsnips	Scrub and pare; use whole or sliced	450 g	3 cups chopped
Pawpaw	Peel and halve, remove seeds, cut as desired	450 g	2 cups
Peaches	Boil to loosen skin, dip in cold water,	3-5 medium	2-2 1/2 cups sliced

Name	Preparation	Quantity	Yield
Peaches (cont'd)	*skin, halve and remove stone, scrape out stone fibres*		
Pears	*Peel thinly to retain pear shape, halve or quarter and core*	*4-5 medium*	*2 2/3 cups sliced*
Pineapple	*Slice off ends, cut into flat rounds, peel and core each ring, cut in wedges if desired*	*1 medium*	*3-3 1/2 cups diced*
Plums	*Remove stems, prick skin to prevent bursting*	*12-20 medium*	*2 cups sliced*
Radishes	*Scrub, cut off root end, use whole or sliced*	*8-10 medium*	*2 cups sliced*
Rhubarb	*Use tender young stalks, trim leaves and ends, cut in 25mm lengths*	*8-12 stalks*	*4 cups diced*
Strawberries	*Use firm, red berries, remove caps*	*3 cups*	*500 ml crushed*
Sweetcorn	*Remove husks and silk with brush, leave cob whole or remove kernels with sharp knife, leaving kernel bases on cob*	*16-20 ears*	*8-10 cups*
Tomatoes	*See p.49*	*4 medium*	*3 cups sliced*

Problems you may encounter	Cause	Prevention
Darkness or discolouration	*(A) Copper, brass, iron or zinc cookware used*	*Stainless steel*
	(B) Chlorinated water used	*Purified water*
	(C) Iodised salt	*Sea salt*
	(D) Powdery, dry spices used	*Fresh or less dry herbs*
Turning brown in jars	*(A) Overcooking or over-ripe produce*	*Bring to boil and remove immediately from heat. Do not overcook.*
Spoilage occurring	*(A) Acidity level too low*	*Vinegar must be 4-6%*
	(B) Jars not airtight	*Check seals and trims before use*
	(C) Hard water	*Purified water*
	(D) Storage area too warm	*Always store jars in cool place*

Preserving Herbs

If you want to use dry organic herbs you will have to learn to preserve your own because few are available commercially. Drying decreases the desirable properties of the herbs, so be sure to preserve them in the right conditions:

1. To conserve desirable properties, plants should be dried in the shade, so as to avoid temperature extremes. Disturb as little as possible during drying process. There are two ways to handle plants:

(A) Spread a thin layer on a clean surface or on paper, or

(B) Hang them in bundles.

Either way, use a dry, well-ventilated place where no moisture or direct sunlight will affect the plants.

NB: Bark is the exception. (See Point 2).

2. For plants, leaves and seeds, dry at temperatures no higher than 25-34°C; for roots, 42° is the limit. Small roots can be dried whole, large ones should be cut lengthwise into pieces and hung up to dry threaded on a string. For bulbs, remove the outer coat, slice and dry not above 38°C. For bark, scrape off outer layer, peel inner layers and dry in direct sunlight.

NB: Berry plants and chillies should be dried in the shade.

3. Plants are properly dried when stems are brittle. Preparing for storage, leaves are usually removed from the stems and stalks, which generally have little value in themselves. The greatest enemies to preserving the effectiveness of dried herbs are light and oxygen. Use dark glass storage containers rather than tins. (For more, see "Keeping An Organic Kitchen — Storage", p.31.)

For information on which parts of the plants of various herbs and spices to use, and their uses, see "Organic Cooking — The Essence of a Meal", p.72-84.

Freezing

Like bottling and preserving, freezing is necessary to enable you to enjoy organic produce all year around. Even though you will lose some of the flavour and nutritional value, you will still retain the advantage of always having food that is free of synthetic chemicals. However, because of this fundamental difference from commercial products, you should be aware that organic food will react differently. In most cases you will use the product immediately after thawing, but with dairy products or bread, for instance, you may want to keep them for several days after thawing. Remember that their life expectancy will probably be about half that of commercial products.

It is important to prepare food properly for freezing, and to mark it clearly so that it is not kept beyond its freezer "life". Never thaw at room temperature.

NB: Thawing meats in water is a widely practised method of speeding up the process. However, this also speeds up the growth of bacteria, so preferably avoid this method or be sure to cook meat thoroughly. Never use frozen foods for raw dishes, such as marinated fish.

Packaging and Storing

As stated in "Keeping an Organic Kitchen — Storage", freezing makes bacteria dormant, it does not kill them. The deterioration process is slowed down. For this reason, it is important to bring food to the freezing level as fast as possible. Frozen food exposed to the air will deteriorate faster, as frost dehydrates the natural juices, therefore storage containers must be airtight.

Strong glass is the best storage material for vegetables, fruits and liquids. Plastic bags, waxed paper or cling film are second-best, as long as they are synthetic chemical free, eg, petrol-based wax, and will obviously be necessary for items such as meat and some vegetables, which will not fit in glass containers.

Plastic containers should not be used for hot liquids, eg, curry sauces, as they may absorb some of the taste, and vice versa. Aluminium containers also are not recommended, as the aluminium will taint food, especially if hot.

When packaging food for freezing, make sure there is no air in the container, such as between the lid and the produce with a glass container. Any air left inside the item will contain moisture, which freezes and turns into frost, the effects of which have already been mentioned and are known as "freezer burn". If using plastic bags, we suggest wrapping the items in cling film first, then place in the bag and take out all the air before sealing. This works especially well with meats and fish.

Fruits and Vegetables

Fruits and vegetables should both be as fresh as possible if intended for freezing. Most vegetables are suitable for freezing, with the exception of some greens, eg, celery, cucumbers, lettuce and radishes. Frozen vegetables are suitable only for cooking, not for salads.

For preparation of vegetables for freezing, refer to chart on "Bottling and Preserving". Most vegetables should be blanched before freezing, as vegetables frozen raw will lose their texture and become chewy. Cut into desired shape for cooking before blanching. Blanch almost to the point of cooking; they will continue to cook while cooling. One vegetable group that should not be blanched before freezing is the pepper family (capsicums, chillies, etc).

Whether blanching or not, vegetables can be frozen in free-flow form by placing prepared vegetables in one layer on trays and then freezing. This is not only convenient, but also retains more nutritional value and suppresses bacterial growth by freezing faster. Once frozen, place in airtight containers for storage. When preparing frozen vegetables for eating, remember you are not cooking them, but reheating them. Frozen vegetables are always best steamed, and if using other methods, cook as little as possible, ie, add last.

Fruits require the opposite treatment; they are best frozen raw, and in most instances whole, eg, strawberries. But in some cases the skin of the fruit may not be wanted on the finished product and it is always best to remove the skin before freezing, eg, for bananas, oranges and avocados. Some fruits will discolour — this can be avoided by using an acid, eg, vinegar, ascorbic acid, lemon juice.

Fruits can be used two ways — frozen for a dessert (eg, ice-cream, milkshakes) or cooked for sauces and jams. Fruits are best frozen in glass jars and in their own juices, to retain the natural flavour and colour, but in most cases plastic bags are acceptable. Fruits can also be frozen in the free-flow method. (See p.58.)

Freezer life

6-8 months.

Thawing

Frozen vegetables should never be thawed before use, as they will lose flavour and texture. The same rule applies to fruits, except when specifically required in thawed form, eg, baking or cold desserts.

Soups and Sauces

When freezing either soups or sauces, it is best to freeze only the liquid part. Soups frozen with vegetables will turn out mushy and with very little flavour. The best way to avoid this is to freeze the broth and add the fresh or frozen vegetables once the soup has been heated. This way you add more flavour and retain nutritional value and texture.

With sauces, freezing will sometimes cause the ingredients to separate when thawing. They can be re-homogenised by using a mixer, food processor or masticator before serving.

Freezer life

6 months.

Thawing

(Time — 8-10 hours)
Soup, broth and cooked sauces should be completely thawed in the refrigerator before heating, to avoid burning.

Red Meat

Red meats generally freeze well. Meat should be frozen without bones and surplus fat, wherever possible. Fat can turn rancid and bones can also affect the flavour of the meat when frozen. Meat should be cut into serving portions before freezing, eg, steaks. Portions should be individually wrapped with cling film and then placed in a plastic freezer bag. The bag must be airtight to insure against freezer burn, which dries out the meat. This applies to both raw and cooked meat.

Frozen steak or topside is safe to cook rare, since any bacteria will be on the surface and will be killed in cooking. Frozen processed meat, such as mince and rolled roasts, can be penetrated by bacteria and must be cooked thoroughly. Casseroles and stews are good for freezing, but leave out any vegetables, rice or pasta. Add these when heating to avoid tasteless mush.

Freezer life

Beef, lamb or veal: 9-11 months whole, 4-6 months processed.
Beef byproducts, eg, liver, kidney: 3-4 months.
Pork (whole or processed): 4-6 months.

Thawing

(Time — 6-15 hours, depending on weight)
Leave wrapped while thawing. Never cook until completely thawed. Thaw in shallow dish at bottom of refrigerator to avoid cross-contamination. Ensure blood from meat does not drip onto vegetables, etc.

Poultry

(Includes chicken, turkey, duck, goose)

When freezing poultry, clean and prepare as if for cooking. Remove all skin and bones, if desired, and cut into serving portions. If leaving whole, ensure all blood and entrails are removed. Wrap in plastic and seal airtight.

WARNING: Poultry is a soft meat and bacteria can move more easily here than in red meat. It is therefore one of the main causes of food poisoning, especially chicken, eg, salmonella. Professional poultry processors blast-freeze their birds, usually as soon as possible after killing. Since blast-freezers are not generally found in the home, it is preferable to freeze poultry in portions rather than whole. Most free-range and organically-reared poultry available in shops has been frozen already, so if you are going to freeze poultry, be sure it has not been frozen before, and that it is as fresh as possible, to avoid bacteria build-up.

Freezer life

9-11 months.

Thawing

(Time — 10-24 hours, dependent on size)

Leave wrapped while thawing. Never cook until completely thawed. Thaw in shallow dish at bottom of refrigerator to avoid cross-contamination. Ensure blood from meat does not drip onto vegetables, etc.

Seafood

Raw seafood to be frozen should always be as fresh as possible. Most fish freeze reasonably well raw, but not cooked. Some shellfish, eg, oysters, mussels and scallops, freeze well raw and reasonably well-cooked, but will tend to be dry. Crustaceans, such as crayfish and crab, freeze best when cooked because they tend to lose texture when frozen raw.

No seafood that has been frozen should be eaten raw or rare. Be sure that any seafood you are freezing has not been frozen before and then thawed for sale.

Fish: Always clean, scale and prepare fish for cooking before freezing, eg, cut into fillets. All fish tends to dehydrate and lose natural juices in the freezer. This occurs less with oily fish, such as tuna and kahawai, and therefore these are your best choice for freezing.

To help avoid dehydration in flaky fish, such as snapper, it is best to wash in a water-salt solution before packaging.

Fish fillets to be frozen should be wrapped individually as airtight as possible. When freezing whole, it is better to use the glazing method. Place unwrapped fish in the freezer after preparation, remove when frozen solid and dip quickly into ice-cold water. This creates a thin coat of ice. Repeat several times until ice coat is about 3 mm thick. Glazing helps to retain the natural juices and avoid dehydration.

Shellfish: Freeze only when raw. Remove shells and wash in a saltwater solution before freezing. Retain solution when packaging in containers or bags. Solution should cover the shellfish.

Crustaceans: These should always be cooked thoroughly in salted water. When cooled, place in plastic bags for freezing.

Freezer life

2-4 months.

Thawing

(Time — 6-10 hours, depending on weight)
All seafood should be thawed in a container in the refrigerator. Remove wrapper as soon as possible and let thaw in liquid to avoid, as much as possible, the natural effects of dehydration.

NB: An alternative to freezing seafood is to place it in a bowl of icy water and leave in the refrigerator. Keep adding fresh ice cubes to the water and the seafood should last for 4-5 days for shellfish and crustaceans, and up to one week for most fish.

Dairy Products

Most dairy products are suitable for freezing, although organic dairy products, such as raw milk, which is not homogenised, will separate into liquid and fat. In this case, after thawing, homogenisation will be necessary to regain the same consistency. This can be done with a food processor, blender or masticator and is best undertaken before the milk is completely thawed.

NB: Milk puddings, custards and jellies tend to curdle during thawing and therefore are not really suitable for freezing.

Freezer life

3 months maximum.

Thawing

(Time — 6-20 hours, approximately or 10 hours per litre)
Thaw at the coldest possible temperature to avoid bacteria growth.

Baked Goods

All baked goods should be frozen as soon as cooked or bought, especially when organic. Uncooked dough tends to lose volume and the texture becomes heavy. This is especially true with organic doughs, and we suggest not freezing them.

Freeze cakes before wrapping — this makes them easier to handle. Wrap all baked goods carefully to avoid freezer burn, as flour is especially vulnerable. Baked goods which are iced, or contain fillings or fruit, do not freeze well.

Freezer life

4-6 months.

Thawing

(Time — 3-8 hours, depending on volume)
Thaw on a tray with draining slats to let the moisture drain away. Eat immediately after thawing. Although baked goods can be thawed in the refrigerator, they are best thawed at room temperature to avoid moisture build-up and sogginess.

CHAPTER FOUR

Organic Cooking

Cooking class, Hukarere Girls' School, Napier, 1913

T he aim of organic cooking is to have control over what we put into our bodies. While organic farming methods are advanced, the cooking methods outlined here effectively turn back the clock to a time before food-processing was a commercial operation. Because of the current lack of commercially-processed, certified organic products, you must become the processor. Like your ancestors, you are doing everything from the baking to the preserving with simple ingredients. This requires some compromise because modern recipes often have ingredients that are commercially available only in chemically-processed forms, or are not available organically.

Commercial food-processing in the 20th century has conditioned consumers to accept enhanced flavours and colours in their food as being normal. For example, most people expect cheese to be yellow because it is processed to this colour. Artificial food colourings and flavourings are essentially cosmetic, ie, they exaggerate the true flavour and colour. This is generally intended to make the products more attractive to the buyer. Turmeric, for example, is used to give mustard its characteristic yellow colour.

Because organic products differ fundamentally from their commercial counterparts, they also need to be treated differently. The first thing you will notice when you start cooking naturally with organic ingredients, is the difference in taste compared with the commercial ingredients used in most recipes. This is because of what has been eliminated from the food. For example, in all-purpose flour you may find emulsifiers, thickeners, stabilisers, etc. All of these affect the final flavour and texture of the food. People eating natural food for the first time often complain that it tastes "bland" because they're used to the artificially-exaggerated flavours which are designed to make processed food taste more "real".

The most commonly used flavour enhancers are salt and sugar and their derivatives. Most people have been conditioned to the "salty" or "sugary" tastes from childhood, but there's a whole range of additives now used commercially to boost flavour beyond that which occurs naturally. The "blandness" people complain about is simply the absence of that high sodium or sugar content. Texture is also an important part of flavour, and many commercial ingredients and foods have texture-influencing ingredients added to them, eg; conditioning agents, emulsifiers, gums, thickeners, stabilisers, surfactants, free-running agents, enzymes and solvents.

The above principles also apply to the different types of processed sugars, such as caster sugar and icing sugar, which are used as flavour enhancers. Sugar is not currently available in organic form, but there are many other alternatives, such as honey, which is available without chemicals.

When converting recipes that call for sugar to honey or another sweetener, many things must be considered. For example, is the finished product going to be a dry item, such as bread; a liquid, such as a sauce; or a glaze, such as the icing on a cake? Is the sugar being used as a preservative, such as in jams? If using honey instead of sugar, simply use half the amount stated.

NB: Mixing honey with vanilla extract is a good substitute for icing sugar. However, you may have to experiment with the amounts, since the icing will not be as firm.

Unlike sugar, alternative sweeteners, such as honey or maple syrup, have flavour as well as sweetness. The flavour will sometimes taste sweeter than sugar, although in fact their sweetness levels are about the same. It is therefore important to select the right sweetener for the recipe in question. For example, if the flavour of the honey would intrude into the overall taste of the recipe, such as ice-cream, use a mild honey, such as clover.

It should also be noted that experimenting with sweeteners can enhance the flavour, such as with some sauces and marinades. When using honey as a glaze or marinade instead of sugar, use the same amount. When making jams and preserves, remember the sweetener will change the flavour.

Unlike sugar, a liquid sweetener will affect the texture of the food. When changing a conventional baking recipe to using a liquid sugar alternative, err on the side of caution, using less rather than more, so the dough doesn't end up too moist.

NB: Honey loses some nutritional value when heated, but will need to be runny for use in some recipes.

Many herbs and spices are available in organic form, but not all of them, and few are available in processed form. A brief explanation of techniques for drying and preserving your own organic herbs and spices is in "How to Eat Organically All-Year-Round — Preserving Herbs".

Your recipes may call for herbs and spices not currently available in organic form, eg, cumin, pepper, paprika and chilli powder. Some of these you can make yourself with our instructions. (See "The Essence of A Meal — Herbs and Spices"), or use the commercial products at your own discretion, deciding what you consider an acceptable level of toxicity by their origin. If your recipe calls for a certain flavour, you may be able to make an organic alternative by breaking it down to the individual ingredients. Curry, for example, is made from a mixture of cumin, turmeric, chilli and coriander seeds. All these ingredients may be available in organic form but you would have to process them. However, in some recipes you will find ingredients that cannot be substituted, such as black pepper. In this case you will have to use the commercial product or go without.

Organic bread is available, but only in a limited variety. If you want to do your own organic baking you'll have to use traditional methods, which take more preparation time than conventional baking products. A large variety of flours are available in organic form. All organic flours will react differently than regular processed flours, which generally contain conditioning agents, such as emulsifiers, even if advertised as "natural". These agents affect the texture and rising qualities of the flour. Natural raising agents are commercially available from health food sources, and while they cannot all be verified as organic, they're about as close as you'll get. Generally they contain bicarbonate of soda, yeast and cream of tartar, and sometimes a light flour, such as corn. Some of these ingredients can be sourced organically, eg, yeast, but as already stated we have not seen a product that gives absolute assurance.

Yeast is the traditional, basic raising agent. In preparing such things as bread, buns or rolls using organic flour, you will need to extend the process of raising and kneading the dough, to ensure it rises properly when baked. In most cases this will involve repeating the raising and kneading three-to-four times, ie, leaving the dough to rise in a warm place, then knocking it back and kneading.

If adapting an old recipe, you'll also need more flour (approximately 25% more) to get the same quantity of finished product, and you'll find it will turn out slightly heavier. This is especially true with biscuits and small cakes.

You've probably noticed that commercially produced wholemeal bread is quite light. This is because a mixture of white and wholemeal flour has been used, usually two-thirds to one-third respectively. For those who prefer their bread white or lighter in texture, unbleached white organic flour is available. It is therefore possible to produce white organic bread without using chemical agents, which are partly the origin of prejudice against white flour. While it can be argued that white flour has less nutritional value, the authors believe eliminating toxic chemicals from our diet is paramount for good health. (For more detailed information, see "Baking" at the end of this chapter.)

Many of your recipes will call for ingredients not available in organic form. Some are available in organic form, such as eggs from free-range chickens, whose feed is supplemented only by organic materials and which are farmed in a synthetic chemical-free environment. As stated before, "Free-Range" does not mean "Organic" (see "Organic Dictionary", p.18) — it only refers to the conditions under which they were raised.

It is a common fallacy that the sign of a healthy egg is a dark yellow yolk. This colour can be artificially controlled by the feed given to the chicken, and there is no scientific visual test to confirm an egg's nutritional value. However, if the white holds together and does not run freely when the egg is broken, this is usually a sign of high protein content. (See also, in this chapter: "Main Courses — Eggs and Dairy Products".)

Condensed and evaporated milk are not natural products — they are highly processed and sweetened, and you will have to substitute them. A good organic substitute for condensed milk is a 50-50 mixture of organic milk and cream, adding honey to taste. However in some cases, eg, ice-cream, quiches, sauces and soups, the raw milk may cause problems with taste and texture because the fat will coagulate. Homogenised milk should be used in such cases, and was about to become available commercially at time of writing. You can homogenise milk yourself using the masticating juicer. (See "Keeping an Organic Kitchen", p.30.)

NB: *Homogenisation should not be confused with pasteurisation, which involves heating the milk and reduces nutritional value. (See "Organic Dictionary".)*

Footnotes From Lance Reynaud

From years of experience in cooking organic foods for thousands of different tastes, I have run into some common complaints associated with natural cooking methods which seem to be easily stereotyped into simple categories:

Complaint	Probable Cause	Answer
Tastes bland	*Person used to high salt level or artificial flavourings*	*Increase spices or try sautéing to increase flavour*
Tastes sour, bitter or bland	*Lack of sweetener*	*Add honey in appropriate quantity*
Baked products heavy or doughy	*Person used to white flour or wholemeal mixed with white flour*	*Use more organic white flour in baking. Ensure dough is properly raised and kneaded*
Vegetables "chewy"	*Person used to well-cooked vegetables*	*Sometimes the fault of the vegetable; cook longer if that's how they want 'em!*
"Doesn't taste like the real thing!", eg, "real" ice-cream, etc	*Person not used to food without artificial ingredients, chemicals and processing*	*Explain why and let them educate their taste buds!*

Cooking Hygiene

When handling any foods, you should always observe some basic rules to avoid contamination. For bacteria growth, the danger temperature zone is 4-60°C. High-risk foods only need to be left in this zone for one-and-a-half hours before they can become unsafe to eat. These include all moist protein foods, such as raw and cooked meats, seafoods, egg and dairy products, cooked meat products (eg, gravies, soups and stocks), cooked vegetables, rice and potatoes.

Anything that lacks acidity (see "Organic Dictionary", p.16), or that you consider perishable, is at risk. Free-range eggs should be checked for contamination before cooking. If boiling eggs, put them in cold water first. If they float, they are not fresh. If breaking the eggs, check for any sign of blood and any strong odour. Raw eggs are a major food poisoner, eg, salmonella. If using eggs raw, such as in mayonnaise, make sure the acidity levels are high enough to eliminate any risk. Always refrigerate any raw egg product.

Raw dairy products have a shorter shelf life than pasteurised equivalents, but in the case of yoghurt, where you have created the bacteria, the shelf life is about the same as the commercial product.

Cooked food which has been refrigerated should be eaten either while cold, or reheated to 83°C. In the case of poultry and rolled roasts, the middle temperature should reach 75-80°C.

Because there are no synthetic fungicides used in organic produce, mould will sometimes form more quickly. This is a localised fungus and usually harmless to humans, if not palatable. Normally it can be cut off and the rest of the product used, at your own discretion. Processed organic foods, such as jams and sauces, also have a shorter shelf life because of the lack of farming chemicals in their raw ingredients. (See "Keeping an Organic Kitchen — Storage", p.31-33.)

*A **general rule:*** If something looks funny, smell it; if it smells funny, get rid of it. Never take a chance!

Extra care should be taken in preparing organically-grown vegetables — some pests will cling and need to be removed by hand. Visually inspect each vegetable before cooking. When using loose-leafed vegetables, such as lettuce, every leaf should be individually washed to ensure no insects remain. Simple soaking will not remove or kill them. Broccoli and cauliflower should be carefully checked as well. Organic potatoes also need special care because of the lack of synthetic herbicides and fungicides which cause them to sprout sooner if stored for any length of time. Before cooking, remove eyes and root sections and cut off any green areas.

NB: *Raw tomatoes are especially at risk from contamination. Beware of very soft tomatoes and those whose skin has burst — they will become a breeding ground for food bacteria.*

When cooking or baking with organic flour and other ingredients, the food should be refrigerated or consumed as soon as possible, as its shelf life will be much less than conventional products because of the lack of preserving chemicals.

When working with different types of food, beware of cross-contamination, eg; raw to cooked meats, or from raw meats to vegetables. This occurs mainly on utensils and cutting surfaces, and also in the refrigerator. (See "Keeping an Organic Kitchen — Storage", p.31-33.)

With pre-frozen foods, always thaw in the refrigerator, not at room temperature. Once frozen foods are thawed, they must be regarded as "At Risk", since this is when bacteria start to grow. For this reason you should not re-freeze thawed food.

Personal hygiene is obviously also an important factor — wash your hands before and after handling foods, and when switching from handling one food item to another, eg, from preparing a meat dish to preparing a dish to be eaten raw, such as a salad. This reduces the risk of cross-contamination. Also avoid coughing or sneezing near food, and don't put your hands near your mouth or face.

THE FIVE MAIN FOOD-POISONING BACTERIA

Type	Source
Salmonella	*Raw meat, poultry, raw milk and eggs*
Staphylococcus aureus	*Human nose, skin, throat* *Cuts and wounds*
Clostridium perfringens	*Raw meat, poultry, vegetables and dried herbs and spices*
Camphylobacter	*Raw meat, poultry and raw milk*
Listeria	*Soil or contaminated water (Kills young and old)*

The Essence of a Meal

The essence of a meal is its flavour. This is derived largely from the various herbs and spices commonly used in cooking. To make sauces, dressings, soups, salads, main courses and desserts 100% organic without sacrificing the traditional flavour expected, you will need to understand how herbs and spices are made, and work. This will enable you to take advantage of the organic herbs and spices available on the market, which may vary from season to season. (For more information, see "How To Eat Organically All-Year-Round — Preserving Herbs", p.56.) ·

When cooking with herbs and spices, one basic rule applies: Use them sparingly to enhance the natural flavour, not to dominate it. Obviously there will be exceptions with exotic or hot, spicy dishes. In dishes with up to six servings, use a half-teaspoon or less of any spice. For herbs, use one-third teaspoon for powder, a half-teaspoon for dry or coarsely-chopped, and one tablespoon for fresh. Dry herbs usually require less because of their concentrated form and sharper flavour. Remember that the best flavours in herbs and spices come from the aromatic oils they contain, and that these will dissipate over time. Some herbs lose these oils, or flavours, more rapidly than others, eg, chervil should be used fresh. Dried herbs and spices should be replaced, and should not be kept longer than one year. (See "Keeping An Organic Kitchen — Storage", p.31-33.)

Dry herbs can be reconstituted by using the liquid to be used in your recipe and letting herbs sit in the liquid for ten minutes or longer. This gives the dry herbs a "fresh flavour" and can be used to substitute if the herbs desired are not available fresh at the time. If sautéing a dish, add any dry herbs during the last 60 seconds of this process for improved flavour. Stir constantly to avoid burning. This is especially good if making Italian sauces, where the oregano and basil can be added to the garlic and onions before the liquid.

If a cooking recipe calls for dry herbs, but you only have fresh and no time to dry, add the fresh herbs during the initial sautéing. This will slightly brown the herbs and imitate that sharper "dry" flavour.

NB: You will need larger quantities of fresh herbs than dry in this case.

The timing and order of the addition of spices is crucial to the final flavour of the recipe. Curries are a good example; the addition of the various flavourings should be divided. Add about a quarter to a third of the spices (curry powder, cumin, turmeric, etc) at the start of cooking, then add the rest towards the finish. This way the curry flavour does not smother everything else — the flavour is more to the outside of the ingredients rather than cooked through them. If adding a fresh product, such as coriander or parsley, add when cooking is done and allow it to be heated by the food unaided. This retains the fresh flavour.

When salt is added, either at the start or finish of the cooking process, it affects the final taste of the meal. An example of this is when cooking beans; the salt can make the beans tough if added at the start of cooking, and impart a salty flavour. Added near the end, the salt remains on the outside, satisfying the need for salt without losing the flavour of the vegetable.

The "heat" generated by certain spices depends on how they are used. Chillies come in a wide variety of shapes, sizes and colours, eg, cayenne, paprika and capsicum, and each can generate "heat" which adds appeal to Asian and Mexican food especially. However, some people don't like their food too "hot", so you need to know how to prepare your "hot" spices accordingly. A fresh chilli will taste different, depending on how it is prepared. In powdered form its flavour will be slightly more concentrated and will depend on the variety and amount used. If used fresh, its "heat" can be increased by frying or grilling on a direct heat. Boiled or oven-baked, it will deliver more flavour than "heat".

You can use combinations of different spices to imitate the flavour of an unavailable spice, eg, curry powder or allspice, or to lower the sugar content of your cooking or baking while still obtaining a "sweet" flavour. Cinnamon, nutmeg and vanilla are all suitable. For further information, see "Common Herbs and Spices" below.

COMMON HERBS AND SPICES

Name	Ingredients and Application
Allspice	*The dried berry of a tropical, evergreen myrtle tree (Caribbean). Can also be made from a blend of cloves (2 parts), cinnamon and nutmeg (4 parts each). Use in cakes, cookies, pies and desserts, pickling, syrups, ethnic stews, roasts and vegetables.*
Anise	*The leaves and seeds of the Pimpinella plant; provides aniseed or licorice flavour. Leaves can be used for salads and crushed seeds for sweets, cookies, cakes and fish sauces.*

74

Basil	*Leaves from the basil plant; use fresh or dry — flavour is similar to mint and cloves combined, and increases with cooking. Because of this, it should be used sparingly. Use with tomato dishes, eg, Italian; also eggs, cheese, salads, meats, fish, sausage mixes, soups and dressings and bland vegetables.*
Bay leaves	*Leaves from the bay tree; use fresh or dry and sparingly — flavour is strong and slightly bitter. For up to eight servings, use one leaf. Use in meat, fish and poultry dishes, stuffings, soups, sauces and marinades, and with bland vegetables.*
Borage	*Leaves and flowers of the borage plant; best used fresh to retain cucumber-like flavour. Fresh leaves used for salads, cold, drinks and fish sauces, or cooked as a vegetable, like spinach. Flowers used for flavour and garnish in punches, iced drinks and salads, and to decorate cakes.*
Capers	*Pickled, unopened flower buds of the caper bush (Mediterranean). Taste like sharp pickles. Use for salads, meat gravies, fish sauces, pizza and other Italian dishes.*
Caraway	*Dried seeds of the caraway plant with a pungent flavour; use in baking, salads, soups, stews, cheeses and sauerkraut.* **NB:** *Flavour is strong and turns bitter with long cooking — add last, eg, in the final 20 minutes for stews.*
Cardamom	*Seeds from the dried fruit of the cardamom plant (India & tropical). Gingerish, leaving a medicinal aftertaste. Use whole (hot punches and wines, marinades, pickling liquids, demi-tasse or regular*

Name	Ingredients and Application
	coffee) or ground (breads, pastries, biscuits and fruit salad). Used in Mexican, Latin and eastern Indian dishes.
Cayenne Pepper	Ground from the dried pods of a small shrub of the capsicum family. The ground pepper is combined with yeast and flour and baked into a hard cake, which is then ground into the finished spice. Can be used instead of black pepper, in a lesser amount, and Indian and Latin cooking, eg, curries and chilli powders. *NB: Cayenne pepper is very hot and should be used sparingly, at say, a ratio of 2-10, compared with black pepper.*
Chervil	Leaves from the chervil plant. Must be used fresh, has a delicate flavour with a slight hint of anise. Use in Continental soups and sauces, salads, omelettes, chicken, veal and fish. *NB: Chervil loses its flavour with prolonged cooking and should be added last.*
Chilli powder	A blend of dried, powdered Mexican chillies and other spices, such as coriander, cumin and oregano. Can be made using dried jalapeno and cayenne (7 parts) and one part each ground dried coriander seeds, cumin and oregano. For a milder recipe with more flavour, use $3^1/2$ parts red capsicum to same amount of chillies withremaining spices. Commercial chilli powder recipes vary widely. Use in Mexican, Asian and Indian dishes.

Chives	*A herb, like the leek and onion. Use fresh or dry for a mild onion flavour in salads, baked potatoes, omelettes, sauces and dips.*
Cinnamon	*The dry inner bark of the evergreen laurel tree. Used in quills (punches, teas, cooked fruit or pickling liquids) or ground (baking, cooked fruits, meat and fish dishes, and desserts).*
Cloves	*Dried unopened flower buds of the tropical evergreen clove tree. Used whole (stewed fruit, hot spiced drinks, pickling liquids and marinades) or ground (baking, fruit dishes, curries and red meat dishes).*
Coriander	*Leaves and seeds of the coriander plant. Dried seeds have a taste of lemon peel and sage. (Use whole in drinks, marinades and pickling liquids; ground in spices, baking and desserts, sauces, curries and other ethnic dishes). Use leaves fresh or dried in meat, poultry, soups and sauces (eg, Latin and Indian) and as a garnish. Also known as Chinese parsley or Cilantro.*
Cumin	*Ground seeds of the cumin plant (Mediterranean). Similar to the caraway seed, but lighter in colour and stronger in flavour. Used in cheese, sauerkraut and other cabbage dishes, barbeque and Italian sauces, chilli and curry powders; also with bland vegetables.*
Curry powder	*A blend of various spices, including cardamom, cayenne, chilli, cloves, coriander, cumin, dill, fenugreek, ginger, mace and turmeric. There are as many different curry recipes as there are curry eaters! (See Curry Powder recipe in this section.) Predominant in Indian and Asian cooking.*

Common Herbs and Spices *(continued)*

Name	Ingredients and Application
Dill	*Leaves and seeds of the dill plant; seeds have stronger flavour. Seeds are used dried (whole or ground) and leaves fresh or dried. Use in cream cheese, sour cream dips, sauces, soups, salad dressings, eggs, pickles and pickling sauces, fish, poultry, sauerkraut, or as a garnish.*
Fennel	*Seeds and leaves of the fennel plant; mild aniseed-like flavour. Dried seeds used in baking, fresh or dried leaves in salads, soups and sauces. NB: Fennel is excellent with seafood, aiding the digestion of oily fish, such as tuna, mackerel and eel. Fresh leaves are preferable to dried.*
Fenugreek	*Dried ground seeds of the fenugreek plant; smells like celery but has a more bitter taste. Mainly used as an ingredient in curries.*
File	*Made from young powdered sassafras leaves; used as a thickening and flavouring in Cajun and Creole cooking.*
Garlic	*Cloves from the garlic plant; used fresh or in dry powdered or flake form. Best used fresh, but will have a stronger flavour when dried. Used commonly as a meat and vegetable seasoning.*
Ginger	*From the root of the ginger plant. Used fresh, peeled and sliced or grated in soups, stews, salad dressings and Asian dishes; can also be rubbed into meats and fishes. Dried ground ginger is used in baking and curries. NB: Dried ginger tends to be more pungent.*

Horseradish	*The root of the horseradish plant. Used fresh and grated, then combined with vinegar and lemon juice (to taste) to make horseradish sauce, or in dried and powdered form as a seasoning in Central European dishes.*
Juniper	*Dried berries of the juniper bush, with a spicy, bittersweet flavour. Used in marinades, cabbage, bean dishes, sauerkraut and as a meat seasoning.*
Leeks	*Member of the onion family, with a sweet flavour. Used dried or fresh in soups, salads and stews or instead of onions. Predominant in French cooking.*
Lemon balm	*Fresh or dried leaves from the balm plant; has a refreshing lemon flavour. Used fresh (in tea, punches and wine), and dry or fresh in salads, sauces, chicken or fish.*
Lemon verbena	*Fresh leaves from the verbena plant; has a lemon flavour. Used in fruit salads, jellies and custard, and as a garnish.*
Lime	*Dried leaves of the lime tree; has a lime-lemon flavour. Used in jellies and custards, but especially in spicy dishes from South East Asia, eg, Gado Gado, or nut butters, or in a sauce for noodles.*
Lovage	*From the lovage plant; flavour like celery, but stronger. Young leaves (fresh or dry) used in sauces, stews, soups and salads. Seeds (crushed or whole) used in cakes, sweets, soups, stews and salads. Stems (blanched) can be eaten like celery or sliced into soups and stews. **NB:** This is a strong herb, and should be used sparingly.*

Common Herbs and Spices *(continued)*

Name	Ingredients and Application
Mace	*Dried outer coating of nutmeg seed. Has similar, stronger flavour. Used in whole or powdered form in baking, cooked fruit and other desserts, or as a seasoning in spicy savoury dishes.*
Marigold	*Fresh or dried petals of the marigold flower; has a subtle taste. Used as a cheap substitute for saffron in seafoods, soups, stews, rice, egg dishes and baking.*
Marjoram	*Fresh or dry leaves of the marjoram plant; has a strong, sweet, sage-like flavour. Prominent in Indian cooking; used in meats, eg, duck, pork, goose and chicken; in dressings and vegetables and as a salad garnish when fresh. **NB:** Use sparingly. Also see "Oreganum".*
Mint	*Fresh or dry leaves of the mint plant; has a fresh, strong flavour which is sharper when dried. Use as a spice for meat, especially lamb, in salads and mint sauce. **NB:** Mint comes in many varieties, including peppermint, spearmint, apple and orange; used in fruit dishes and drinks.*
Mustard	*Leaves and seeds of the black and white mustard plant. The condiment is made from dried, powdered seeds mixed with water, vinegar or wine. The dry powder is used to flavour all types of savoury dishes. The whole seeds are used in pickling, sausages and vegetable dishes. Fresh leaves of the white plant can be cooked as a vegetable alone or added to other vegetable dishes.*

Nasturtium	Fresh leaves and flowers of the nasturtium plant; has a peppery flavour similar to watercress. Used in salads, or chopped in cheese sauces and dips. The unripe seed pods can be pickled and used as a for capers.
Nutmeg	The dried kernel from the seed of the nutmeg tree. Used freshly-grated in desserts, baking, stewed fruits, drinks and savoury dishes. **NB:** Use sparingly.
Oreganum	Fresh or dried leaves of the wild marjoram plant (Oreganum vulgare); has a flavour sharper and spicier than marjoram. A prominent ingredient in Italian and Latin dishes, but has many other applications. A regular companion to garlic.
Paprika	From the dried pepper pods of the largest and mildest capsicum shrub. (See also "Cayenne" and "Chilli Powder".) Used in many dishes to add colour and flavour, especially spicy stews, such as goulash.
Parsley	Fresh or dried leaves of the parsley plant; has a mild, savoury flavour which boosts bland food. Used extensively in many dishes, but especially as a garnish. Mixes well with other herbs.
Pepper	The dried berries of the tropical pepper vine, black peppercorns coming from the cured under-ripe berries, white from the ripe berries whose dark outer shell has been removed. Black pepper is stronger, but white has a more aromatic flavour. Best freshly ground. Black pepper is used to enhance all savoury foods, white for lighter-tasting sauces.

Common Herbs and Spices *(continued)*

Name	Ingredients and Application
Poppy seeds	*Seeds from the corn poppy; used as a savoury topping for biscuits, breads and rolls, also sprinkled on salads and vegetables.*
Rose	*The fruit (hip) and flower petals of the rose bush; used for drinks and enhancing jellies and other fruit dishes.*
Rosemary	*Fresh or dried leaves of the rosemary shrub; has a pungent, pine-like, sweet taste. Used in meats, fish, chicken and some green vegetables.* **NB:** *Use sparingly.*
Saffron	*Leaves of the saffron plant; a delicate and expensive flavour — substitutes often used. (See "Marigold" and "Turmeric".) Used in small quantities in rice and seafood dishes, poultry and baking. Can also be used as a digestive aid in oily meat dishes, such as pork, duck and goose.*
Sage	*Fresh or dried leaves of the sage plant; has a delicate, minty flavour when fresh, pungent and aromatic when dried. Great with all meats, especially in stuffings, and with egg and cheese dishes. Makes oily dishes, eg, pork, duck, goose, mackerel or eel seem lighter.* **NB:** *Use sparingly and add last to avoid bitterness.*
Sesame seeds	*Seeds of the sesame plant which have a sweet, nutty flavour. Used toasted or fresh in baking, vegetables and casseroles.* **NB:** *Toasting before use sharpens the taste.*

Shallots	*Branch of the onion family; have a subtle flavour. Used in French dishes and as an accompaniment to meat and poultry.*
Sorrel	*Fresh leaves of the sorrel plant; have a slightly sour taste. Used in salads, vegetable dishes (especially cabbage) and soups.*
Sweet cicely	*Fresh or dry leaves of the cicely plant (North America); has a sweet anise-like flavour. Used on desserts, in juices, salads and soups, or anywhere a sweetener is required as a sugar substitute. Can be used liberally.*
Tarragon	*Fresh or dry leaves of the tarragon shrub; has a licorice flavour with a sweet-sour taste. Important in French cooking, used in egg salads, sauces, fish, meat and poultry dishes, and is also excellent in vinegars. Best fresh, or preserved in vinegar.*
Thyme	*Fresh or dry leaves of the thyme bush; one of the strongest herbs, with a pungent clove-like flavour. Used widely in Mediterranean cooking, sprinkled over meat, fish and poultry, in cheese, egg and vegetable dishes, and in dressings and stuffings. Stimulates appetite and helps digestion. Use sparingly.*
Turmeric	*From the dry root of a plant in the ginger family; has a bitter, gingery taste. Used mainly in small quantities to give golden colour to curries, mustards, mayonnaises, pickles and sauces. A substitute for saffron.*

Common Herbs and Spices *(continued)*

Name	Ingredients and Application
Vanilla	*Dry pods of the vanilla vine (usually known as vanilla beans), fermented and cured six months before use; has a strong sweet flavour — use sparingly. Extract made by soaking beans in alcohol solution, but you make your own by simply soaking a vanilla bean in your favourite alcohol, eg, brandy, vodka,etc. Flavour will improve with age. Used as a sweetener and in desserts.*
Watercress	*Grass-like plant. Fresh leaves may be used in salads, raw or deep-fried, or added chopped to egg, cheese and fish dishes.*

Sprouting

Sprouted produce is traditionally regarded as being rich in nutritional value — its use is documented well back into the BC era. Organic produce is especially suitable for sprouting because you can be sure the seeds or grains were not treated with synthetic chemicals, such as fungicides and pesticides. Commercially grown seeds may have been sprayed before planting, the grains after harvesting. Certified organic products for sprouting are guaranteed free of synthetic chemicals, either in the parent plant or source, or at any point during growing and harvesting.

Be careful you don't defeat the whole purpose by using ordinary tap water or soaking them in an aluminium container! Tap water can contain chlorine, fluoride, aluminium and sediment from the pipes. Always use purified water (see "Keeping an Organic Kitchen — Water Purifier", p.28) when soaking seeds or grains for sprouting.

84

Containers for soaking and sprouting should be made of glass, stainless steel or unbleached cardboard, preferably organic. Avoid using metal mesh screens when draining, as these can contain aluminium. Use an unbleached, preferably organic, thin cotton or muslin cloth instead. Any wholegrain, bean or seed can be sprouted. These include wheat, oats, barley, rye, lentils, soya, alfalfa seeds and chickpeas. For information on availability of organic goods for sprouting, see "How To Eat Organically All-Year-Round — Product Availability", p.41-44.

Sprouting Methods

(1) For sprouting grains (eg, wheat, oats, corn)

- Wash, place in a jar and cover with water (2 tbsp of grain in a litre-size jar will give you enough for a loaf of bread).
- Soak overnight, then drain.
- Cover the jar with a cloth for draining and breathing purposes. Secure with an Agee collar or rubber band and turn upside down in sink to drain remaining water. Then leave in a dark, cool place for 2-3 days, rinsing at least twice a day.
- Once a root approximately 50mm long appears, place in direct sun light for 2-3 hours. This allows chlorophyll to develop and increases nutritional value.
- Then put into covered glass container and use as soon as possible. Refrigerator life is about five days.

(2) For sprouting seeds (eg, alfalfa, sesame)

- Use the same method as above and place in refrigerator.
- If you want shoots, eg, alfalfa for eating raw, after the root appears, place the jar in a cool, lighted room out of direct sunlight.
- Let grow to desired length, then refrigerate (five days maximum).

NB: You may want to add a little water to the jar during growing period, to avoid drying out, especially during summertime. The usual growing period after the root appears is one to one-and-a-half weeks. If sprouting in larger quantities, a tray can be used.

(3) For sprouting beans (eg, mung, chickpeas and pinto)

- Use the first method, but allow 3-6 days for the root to appear.
- Most larger hard beans will require 24 hours of soaking and should be rinsed at least three times a day after draining.
- Smaller, softer beans, eg, mung, usually react the same as seeds whether sprouting or shooting.
- If using beans for cooking you will find it easier to sprout them in the cooking container because of the larger quantity involved.
- If using beans for baking you will require approximately one-eighth of a cup for one loaf of bread.
- If bean sprouts are desired, after the root appears, place on a tray lined with a damp cloth and store in cool, lighted area away from direct sunlight. Leave until sprouts of desired length appear, keeping cloth damp.
- Beans take longer to sprout than seeds. After they reach desired length, refrigerate no longer than five days.

(4) Nuts (eg, almonds)

Some nuts swell up when sprouting, rather than developing a root, and break open to produce the shoot.

- They should only be soaked for 24 hours.
- Use in salads, cooking and baking.

Grains, seeds and beans, when sprouted for the root only, are normally used for cooking or baking, in dishes such as soups, casseroles, stir-fries and bread. Do not waste the initial water used for soaking and sprouting — this retains nutritional value and should be used in the baking or cooking process, or as a base for other dishes, such as soups and stews. Fully-sprouted products are more commonly eaten raw, eg, in sandwiches and salads, but some can be used in stir-fries, eg, mung beans and grains.

Soups, Sauces and Dressings

In these weight-conscious days, people tend to be more selective when consuming soups, sauces and dressings. They are wary of "heavy" recipes, ie, where the liquid is thick, either because of the high fat content or because they are intolerant of dairy or flour products. These are frequently used as thickeners in commercial soups, sauces and dressings. The organic versions are scarce, and you will need to be able to make your own. This, however, should be seen as an opportunity to create interesting dishes using wholly organic ingredients, eliminating thickening agents you might not want in your diet.

A food processor or high-speed blender is an essential tool for making thick soups, sauces and dressings. A thick vegetable soup, for example, can be made using bland, starchy vegetables such as potatoes, which will require processing. (See "Recipes" later in this chapter.) A consommé is a thin broth made by boiling and straining meat and/or vegetables, etc. If using organic products to make your consommé, be sure to use purified water in the boiling process. The basis of a consommé is the stock which will provide the essential flavour — meat, poultry, seafood, vegetable, etc.

A well-presented meal is more appetising, especially if introducing someone to organic food! Sauces and dressings are usually added last before serving, and are important to the overall presentation of the meal. The final touch is garnishing — adding fresh herbs, vegetables, etc, to enhance the appearance and flavour. The art of food presentation and garnishing lies in ensuring taste is not sacrificed for appearance.

A crowded plate not only looks messy, it spoils the flavours of the meal because all the ingredients tend to get mixed together, whether you want them that way or not. Be sure the plate is a good size, even for side dishes, and position the food on the plate so the diners can see everything that is being put in front of them.

If serving a rice or pasta dish, pour the sauce into the centre — make a depression in the middle with a spoon or ladle first. That untouched outer rim of rice or pasta looks much more attractive and allows people to take as much sauce as they please.

Large tossed salads are fine for barbecues or large gatherings, but if serving individual salads, bunch each vegetable together (you can make eye-catching arrangements), then gently pour the dressing between the ingredients, rather than drowning them in it. Garnish should also not be hidden, even if it is not necessarily to be eaten, and always try to use organic garnish, such as parsley. Simple is always best, so don't over-garnish your dishes. A twist of citrus fruit or a julienne (stick cut) of a hard vegetable, such as carrot, celery or radish, is often enough.

Preparation

The main differences when preparing organic soups, sauces and dressings lie in the reaction of organic ingredients, and in replacing non-organic ingredients. Organic spices, for example, are limited in their variety and you may have to seek alternatives. The availability of organic ingredients is detailed in other chapters. Honey or another organic sweetener may need to be used instead of sugar, which is not available yet in organic form.

Organic milk will need homogenising in a masticator or blender (see "Keeping an Organic Kitchen — Appliances", p.28) to avoid getting fatty globules if you're after a creamy dish. You can strain it through a sieve, but this will make the milk watery and probably defeat the purpose of using it in the first place. It is worth noting here that a food processor's action heats whatever it is processing by friction. Use this to your advantage by adding some vegetable ingredients to the processor in their raw form, eg, spring onions, carrots or

celery, for a better taste.

If you are eliminating dairy products or flour from your diet, but want a thick or creamy product, there are several alternatives available. With soups and sauces, either use less water in the cooking process or strain and retain the liquid after cooking. Manual "mashing" of ingredients before placing in the processor will give you a thicker product, due to less time being spent in the machine.

If the recipe gets too dry, add water or the liquid you have retained from cooking. If using whole vegetables as part of a recipe, eg, vegetable soup, cook the whole vegetables separately and add to the other ingredients after processing. As mentioned before, a starchy vegetable such as potato can also be used as a thickener. Boil them, mash them, process them, then add them to the other ingredients. Tofu can be used as a substitute in soups, sauces or dressings that call for eggs or dairy products, such as cream or cheese. It can also be used half-and-half with dairy products or eggs to retain the flavour but lower the cholesterol or fat level. Tofu also has a higher protein level. Most soup recipes call for stock, usually in cubes, which is not readily available in organic from. Therefore you will have to make your own, which always ßtastes better than those processed, dehydrated cubes. (See "Cooking Methods" on the next page.)

Sauces basically fall into four categories: Roux, emulsion, sweet and mayonnaise. Roux sauces are either white, using milk or cream, or brown, using flour. The most common brown roux sauce is gravy. Emulsion sauces are of a delicate flavour and made from butter and eggs, eg, hollandaise. Most emulsion sauces require clarified butter, which you will have to make yourself since it is not available in organic form.

To do this:
- Place butter in a heat-proof container and stand in a pan of hot water over a low heat.
- When the butter has melted, pour off the oily substance from the top and discard the milky sediment below.
- The oily residue is clarified butter, which you can use immediately or store in the refrigerator for later.

Unfortunately for those who do not eat eggs, there is no real organic substitute for these in sauces and dressings where egg whites are needed for thickening. As mentioned in the "Main Courses" section, p.112-113, organic eggs display a better thickening quality due to their extra protein. A recipe calling for egg whites as a thickener will require less whites, or better still, use the whole egg for complete nutritional value.

Sweet sauces are most often used in desserts, and the sweetener used most often is sugar, which is not available at present in organic form. Alternatives include honey, vanilla, maple syrup or fructose. Remember all these alternatives will react differently to sugar because they are available only in liquid form. You may want to reduce other liquid ingredients to compensate in your recipe. A mixture of honey and vanilla provides the closest taste to sugar — use 2 parts vanilla to 8 parts honey.

Mayonnaise is not available in processed organic form at present, and we prefer home-made mayonnaise to commercial — fresh is always best. You can obtain all the ingredients in organic form, and we modestly believe the recipe in this book (see "Recipes", p.161) is outstanding! The basic mayonnaise recipe can be either a sauce or a dressing and has infinite variations, eg, tartare, Thousand Island.

FOOTNOTE: *The most commonly used sauce — tomato — is available commercially in organic form. However, a tomato sauce recipe is included in the "Recipes", p.160, section for those who wish to make their own basic tomato sauce, or an exotic variation.*

Cooking Methods

Soups, sauces and dressings are always better cooked at a low heat, stirring constantly to avoid burning, and should be kept covered during cooking to retain flavour and moisture. Be sure to follow the order for adding ingredients stated in the recipe — this is to ensure the right texture.

Whether making a thick or thin soup, you may require a stock first.

For a meat stock, eg, beef or chicken:
- Boil the meat first for 30-40 minutes, allow to cool, then place in refrigerator until the fat has solidified on the surface. This allows for easy removal of the fat.
- After removal of fat, strain off the liquid.
- In a pot, sauté onion, carrot, parsnip and celery in butter until soft.

For beef stock, add raw tomato.
- Add strained liquid, along with pepper, salt and spices to taste.
- Simmer for two hours at low heat, strain off the stock and either use immediately, refrigerate or freeze.

An organic vegetable stock requires a little more ingenuity. You may not be able to obtain all the vegetables in season at the right time, so you may have to compromise with others that are similar in taste.

To make a vegetable stock:
- The basic ingredients are garlic, onion, capsicum, parsley and celery.
- Sauté first in vegetable oil for proper flavour until soft, then add water and peeled potatoes, carrots and tomatoes (or any variations).
- Add salt, pepper and spices to taste, then simmer for about 90 minutes.
- Cool and then place in refrigerator until oil rises to the surface. As much of this oil as possible must be separated from the stock to avoid an oily texture. You should try to disturb the stock as little as possible when separating the oil — use a spoon or ladle.
- Heat the stock again and run it through a sieve — by this point the liquid should have reduced by half. Use immediately or refrigerate.
- If a creamy product is desired, run through a food processor rather than separating the oil and the liquid.

Cooking a meat or vegetable in its sauce will give you only the taste of the sauce. Cooking the sauce separately and adding it afterwards means you get both flavours. If baking a dish with its sauce, eg: rice, macaroni or lasagne, mix the sauce and other ingredients when hot just before placing in the oven — the effect should be to grill rather than to cook again.

Cooking Times

Soups or sauces should be cooked no longer than 35 minutes after reaching boiling or simmering point (45 minutes for 500 grams of meat) — overcooking destroys flavour and nutritional value. Dressings will require much less time because of their delicate flavour.

Some recipes may call for long, slow cooking. Try to reduce this time by cooking some ingredients separately and then adding them to the recipe towards the end of the overall cooking time. A bean soup, for instance, may require the beans to be cooked first, ie, longer than the vegetables.

A tip: *The flavours of meat, seafood or vegetables, used in a sauce or soup, will stand out if cooked by themselves first and then added just prior to serving. This technique applies equally to most cooking styles and ingredients, avoiding a confusion of flavours that ends up tasting like nothing in particular.*

Main Courses

When you buy organic food, you benefit through having food not only free of synthetic chemicals, but of higher nutritional value than its non-organic counterparts. The best way to achieve full flavour and maximum nutritional value from your food is to keep cooking time to a minimum.

When preparing to cook a new recipe or changing an old one to organic ingredients, carry out all prepping (cutting, chopping, etc) before turning on the stove. This will avoid burning and will allow you time to concentrate on cooking.

Sauces should usually be prepared before the actual meal where they are to be used.

Follow cooking instructions and don't cut corners — there's always a reason, usually to do with the final flavour of the dish. However, once you have mastered a recipe, you should feel free to improvise when you believe you can make improvements. One way you can do this is by by cooking some ingredients separately. For example, if a sauce recipe requires garlic and onions, sauté them separately, then add to the finished sauce. This separates the flavours, and the concept can be applied infinitely.

Another tip: *If using dried herbs in a recipe requiring sautéing, it is a good idea to add the herbs at this stage, to revive the original flavour. Using variations like these and experimenting with cooking instructions, such as quantities and order of ingredients, will help you develop tasty cooking secrets of your own, making your meals unique and turning you from a cook into a chef!*

Meats

As the old saying goes, "We are what we eat". Organically reared animals will produce meat with a different taste from their commercial counterparts. This should be considered a desirable quality, along with the usually lower fat content that comes from free-ranging and a more diverse diet.

Synthetic chemicals, antibiotics and "formula" feeds will usually speed up the animal's growth and allow it to be kept in an unnatural environment, eg, battery hens. But, according to Dr George Curlin of the US National Institute of Allergy and Infectious Diseases, "The more you use antibiotics, the more rapidly Mother Nature adapts to them".

Antibiotics give the animal artificial protection from bacteria, so more of its energy is devoted to producing, ultimately, a bigger carcass. However, the bacteria in the animal can become immune to the antibiotics, and these bacteria then can be passed on to humans who drink milk or eat meat from these animals. This acquired immunity deficiency is being partly blamed for the upsurge of such infections as Streptococcus A, tuberculosis and cholera, which are becoming more immune to existing antibiotics. The meat is likely to retain the properties and even the taste of those chemicals.

By contrast, any organic food supplements given to the animals will enhance flavour and nutritional value. All meats, like vegetables, lose nutritional value the longer they are cooked. However, some meats require thorough cooking to ensure they are free from bacteria.

Red Meats

Preparation

Trim away excess fat and remove bones if possible. Cut across the grain of the meat — if cutting with the grain, the meat will turn out chewy or stringy. If using organic mince, whether in patties or loaves, you will need to add more flour and moisture to stop the mince from breaking up. This is because organic meat has less fat, which binds the meat together and imparts an oily texture.

Organic meats have the same shelf life as regular meats, but all meats should be cooked as soon as possible if bought fresh, for nutritional and hygienic reasons.

Cooking Methods — In Order of Preference

Rotisserie is considered one of the best methods of cooking any meat. Sometimes referred to as a "dry cooking method", it involves rotating the meat on a spit over an open flame or heat, allowing the natural juices and fat to drip into the flame and return as moisture into the meat. This ensures tenderness and lower fat content, since the meat is not sitting in its own fat while cooking.

Barbecuing/Grilling is sometimes referred to as char-broiling (North America). Similar to the rotisserie method, the meat is on an open grill with the heat or flame usually underneath, once again allowing the meat juice to drop onto the flame and return as steam. (Sometimes this method is reversed, with the heat above.)

This method requires extra care, especially with the placing of the meat and the height of the grill, to ensure meat is cooked properly inside without burning the outside.

NB: Untreated wood is preferable fuel to charcoal, which will taint the flavour of the food and may contain toxic chemicals. If using gas, be sure that all the vapours are being burnt off properly and not being absorbed into the meat. (See "Keeping An Organic Kitchen", p.29.)

Hangi cooking, where the meat is steamed slowly over heated stones in a covered pit, retains flavour.

NB: *Most modern hangis use aluminium foil to wrap meat, which can taint it. The traditional method of wrapping in leaves, eg, flax or banana, is preferable and gives added flavour.*

Frying, roasting, pot-roasting, oven-grilling, braising, stewing and casseroling all involve the meat cooking in its own juices.

These are less preferable cooking methods because the finished product will have a higher fat content. Sometimes stewing or casseroling are necessary when using tougher cuts of meat.

Cooking Times

Overcooked meat loses its nutritional value, but not cooking for long enough can increase the risk of food poisoning. Red meat, unlike poultry, is generally firmer and more resistant to bacteria, which tends to gather only on the outside surface. This is why it is safe to eat a rare steak, where only the outside has been cooked.

Because organic meat is lean, it can lose its juices more easily when cooking. If well-done meat is desired, organic meat should be covered while cooking to avoid losing essential juices.

Red meat can also be eaten raw if marinated properly in an acidic solution, eg, vinegar or lemon. However, pork, minced meat and rolled roasts should all be well-cooked to ensure all bacteria are killed. (See "How to Eat Organically All-Year-Round — Freezing", p.57-63.) Pork, like poultry, should be thoroughly cooked and never eaten raw or rare. Lamb, on the other hand, should never be overcooked and should be pink at the bone. Although tradition sometimes decrees otherwise, all meat byproducts, eg, liver and sweetbreads, should be well cooked, given modern knowledge that bacteria grow faster in soft, moist meats.

The following are general guidelines for cooking times.
Beef — *Rare: 7-12 minutes per 500gms at 180°C; Medium: 15-18 minutes per 500 g at 180°C; Well Done: 28-32 minutes 180°C.*
Lamb — *Rare: 12-16 minutes per 500 g ; Medium: 20-22 minutes per 500 g.*
Pork and Veal — *Well Done: 30-35 minutes per 500 g .*

Processed and cured meats

Sausages are the most commonly eaten processed meat, and a large selection of organic sausages is now available. These will generally contain less fat than normal sausages because the meat is leaner, but the overall content of the sausages (fat, breadcrumbs, suet, etc) is up to the individual butcher.

When buying organic sausages, be sure that the term "organic" applies to all the contents, and to the casings. Organic processed and cured meats, such as salami and pastrami, will have no preserving chemicals used either in raising or processing and therefore will have a shorter shelf life, even when refrigerated. Keep raw sausages no longer than three days in the refrigerator. Whole cured sausage, such as salami or pepperoni, should not be kept in the cold part of the refrigerator as this will cause mould to form. They should preferably be stored in the vegetable crisper or the door compartments. Some people prefer to hang these in a cool, dry area.

Other cured meats, such as pastrami, are usually bought sliced and therefore are more vulnerable to bacteria. Keep in the cooler part of the refrigerator. All sliced organic meats, including sausage, should be stored wrapped in paper to retain moisture. Their shelf life will be approximately half that of the non-organic product.

Preparation

Do not prick the skin of organic sausages before cooking, as this will drain the juices from them and cause them to lose shape. Cook whole, turning to ensure the outside is cooked all the way around, then make two diagonal slices in each end of the sausage. This is a more effective way of releasing fat than pricking, and ensures the inside is cooked without the outside getting burned.

Cooking Methods — In order of preference

Barbecuing or grilling is preferred but other methods previously mentioned are all acceptable cooking methods for sausages. Because of the generally lower fat content of organic sausages, it may be necessary to add a little oil or fat to avoid sticking.

Cooking Times

- 12 minutes on a hot barbecue
- 20 minutes in oven grill or pan
- All other methods (eg, boiling, steaming) — 20 minutes.

If using cured meats, eg, salami on a pizza, the aim should be heating only and not overcooking, as cured meat becomes tough very quickly. Always add as late as possible.

Poultry

Preparation

Make sure all feathers or small hairs have been removed. Chicken and turkey are leaner poultry and are easier to digest. The small amount of fat these birds contain is mostly found under the skin, and usually around the area known as the "Parson's Nose" (tail flap). If not wanted, the skin and fat in this area should be removed before cooking.

Stuffing made from organic bread should be prepared as close to cooking time as possible, and should not be put into the bird more than an hour before cooking. Remember, organic flour is usually heavier and retains more moisture — you may want to make your mixture a little drier than normal, as it will absorb the fluid from the bird.

The white meat (eg, the breast) is lowest in fat; the darker meat (eg, the legs) has more. Never break up cooked poultry meat with your fingers if using for pies, sandwiches or salads, as it will break with the grain and the meat will be stringy and tough. Always cut with a knife across the grain.

Cooking Methods — In Order of Preference

Refer to the "Red Meat" section.

NB: *Most free-range chickens are roasting birds less than one year old. Anything older is normally known as a boiling fowl.*

Because free-range chicken contains less fat it has less juice, and you may need to add a little liquid if cooking in a pan, to avoid drying out. Other poultry, such as ducks and geese, have less meat and more fat. If cooking these with the skin on, it should be pricked all over to allow some of the fat juices to escape during cooking.

The main meat area on these birds is the breast. If glazing free-range chicken with any sauce, you may need more liquid to avoid drying out or burning, again because of the lower fat content.

Cooking Times

Poultry should always be cooked thoroughly because as a soft meat, it is especially vulnerable to food poisoning bacteria. No red or pink meat should be visible near the bone.

- Chicken: 20-25 minutes per 500 g at 180°C.
- Turkey: 35 minutes per 500 g at 145°C (Turkey requires slow cooking to ensure the meat cooks right to the bone without burning the outside.)
- Goose and Duck: 18-25 minutes per 500 g at 180°C.

To ensure the bird is cooked properly, stick a knife into a thick part of the meat, such as the thigh, right to the bone. If any red juice emerges, it needs more cooking.

Seafood

Seafood is usually considered free-range, not a farm product. But this is increasingly far from true, as more and more seafood is being farmed today, eg, mussels, salmon and prawns. In the process, pesticides, chemical food, antibiotics and even colouring are used in the farming and processing.

With seafood, you should always be sure of the source. Some seafood farmers say their product is "raised in pollution-free waters", which may be true but does not indicate how they were reared.

At time of writing, we know of only one certified organic seafood produced in New Zealand — salmon which is solely for export. So when buying seafood, reject the farmed variety to avoid unnecessary synthetic chemicals in your diet.

When purchasing fish, remember they come in two categories: smooth-skinned and scaly. Smooth-skinned fish tend to be scavengers or bottom feeders (eg, sharks and flounder), while scaly fish are not natural scavengers and are a safer choice if eating raw.

It is better to know the source of shellfish, and that it is free of toxins, because no amount of cooking or acidity will kill these. In fact, toxins can thrive in heat! Shellfish tend to proliferate in shallow coastal waters which are more vulnerable to pollution and infestation (eg, toxic algae). It is better to select crustaceans sourced from the deep sea for the same reason.

Preparation

All scaling, gutting and boning (if necessary) should always be completed before cooking. Wash fish thoroughly after these preparations. If desired, remove head, fins and tail before cooking. Use cooking scissors rather than a knife for removing fins.

When preparing shellfish, remove flesh from shell along with inedible matter, eg, the beard and attached muscle in mussels. Crustaceans, such as prawns, have an intestinal cord, usually running along the spine to the tail — it is blue-coloured in some species. This should be removed before cooking, along with the stomach contents of crustaceans, as these can contain bacteria. Do not leave unprepared raw seafood lying out in the open — keep in the refrigerator and covered until use.

Cooking Methods – In Order of Preference

Grilling and steaming are the two best methods for cooking seafood, since neither uses oil or butter and therefore is lower in fat. Grilling is the best way to get maximum flavour and nutritional value from fish steaks. Steaming (eg, a hangi) or poaching is especially suitable for more delicate fish, such as John Dory, or for special diets.

Fillets are best pan-fried or baked since they lack a bone and may need a little extra moisture, such as oil or butter, to keep from drying out and flaking. If pan-frying skinned fish, use a coating, such as flour or egg and breadcrumbs, to help seal in the moisture and protect from the extreme heat.

Otherwise, fry in a hot pan as quickly as possible. Whole fish can be cooked in any of these ways, or boiled for soups and stews.

Oily fish (eg, kahawai, trout and tuna) are very suitable for baking because they do not dry out so quickly. Shellfish and crustaceans can be steamed, boiled or baked in or out of their shells, fried shelled whole or minced, or grilled/barbecued in their shells.

Smoking is generally done to preserve fish as well as impart a different flavour. If smoking your own fish, be sure the wood you are using is not from treated timber, as this contains poisonous chemicals. Manuka is the best choice for smoking in New Zealand — do not use pine, as it contains resins that will taint the fish. You can smoke fish either whole or in fillets. Roes and shellfish are also good smoked.

The preferred method is to use three or four small lumps of wood. Allow these to smoulder gently underneath the fish with the vents of the smoker open to let in oxygen during cooking. This process should take approximately two hours. Then close vents and cover the wood with either sawdust or green wood for the curing process, which imparts the characteristic colour to the outer flesh. This should take approximately four hours. Remember it is the smoke you want, not heat. The smoke contains formaldehyde, a natural preservative which hardens the flesh. The acids in the smoke also kill bacteria.

Allow the fish to cool after smoking before storage. Smoked fish will keep almost indefinitely, but a year is probably the maximum. If storing in the refrigerator, keep the fish in brown paper or an airtight container rather than plastic, as this can cause it to sweat and bacteria or mould to form.

Eating raw seafood such as fish, prawns, octopus, kina and shellfish can be dangerous, unless it is marinated in an acidic solution (eg, vinegar or lemon juice). "Raw" fish has different names around the world, eg, Sushi (Japan), Ceviche (Latin America), but the preparation is roughly similar. Dice the flesh and steep in acidic solution for roughly six hours or overnight in the refrigerator, stirring occasionally. (Refer to "Recipes" for Ceviche, p.156.) If using crustaceans or shellfish, remove shells before steeping. With crustaceans, use smaller-sized prawns or chop flesh of larger types, such as crayfish or lobster, and proceed as before. Prepare octopus or squid as you would other fish.

Cooking Times

The line between cooking and overcooking seafood is very thin; going over the line can leave it dry, chewy, tasteless and lacking in nutritional value. On the other hand, undercooking leaves the flesh gelatinous in texture and bland in taste.

- Pan-fry fish no longer than 8 minutes, depending on thickness.
- Bake no longer than 10-25 minutes in a hot oven.
- Crustaceans should be fried no longer than 5 minutes and baked in the shell for 10-25 minutes.
- Shellfish in the shell should be steamed or baked only until the shells open, or for up to 10 minutes.
- If frying the meat, cook no longer than 5 minutes.
- If boiling any seafood, cooking times will vary greatly depending on use, eg, soup, broth, sauce or stew. All seafood should be cooked for at least 5 minutes if boiling.
- Fish and crustaceans should be grilled or barbequed for no more than 10-12 minutes.
- Shellfish can be grilled or barbequed for 10-15 minutes or until shells open.

As stated before, nutritional value is reduced the longer the cooking time. If taste and texture are more important, cooking time will be longer. For more nutritional value, add the seafood last. Overcooking will make shellfish and crustaceans tough and chewy.

Vegetables

More and more people today are switching to vegetarian or semi-vegetarian diets, for a variety of reasons. For those who opt for eating more vegetables on health grounds, it is important to realise that the benefits of a vegetarian diet can be reduced if you eat non-organic produce.

Eating organic vegetables raw is the best way to obtain maximum nutritional value, and because they are free of toxic chemicals they are especially good for salads. But due to strict New Zealand agricultural laws, most fresh organic produce cannot be imported, since it would have to be sprayed with synthetic chemicals. Organically grown produce, therefore, is subject to seasonal availability in this country, and you will need to preserve some items yourself if you want to eat them all-year-round. (See "How To Eat Organically All-Year-Round — Preserving and Bottling".)

Organic vegetables deteriorate faster than conventionally grown produce because they have not been treated with synthetic herbicides, pesticides or fungicides. (For more information, see "Keeping an Organic Kitchen — Storage", p.31-33.) Refrigeration robs vegetables of their taste and texture, and they are best kept in a cool place and consumed as soon as possible. Ripening of vegetables, eg, tomatoes, is best done outside the refrigerator as well, to ensure even maturing. Vegetables are best consumed when just approaching the peak of ripeness; after that, they start to lose texture and nutritional value.

Beans come in two varieties: Hard (pinto, chickpea, lentil) and soft (green peas or beans, mung). Hard beans must be either cooked or sprouted to be eaten (see "Sprouting", p.84-85), while soft beans can be eaten raw, sprouted or cooked.

Processed vegetable products, such as tofu or tempeh, which are made from soy beans, are cooked during processing and therefore will require less cooking time, as you will be just heating for flavour. However, you should check any "flavoured" tofu or tempeh products to see what was added.

A wide variety of seafood vegetables is also available in raw dried or powdered form, eg, arame, nori and hijiki. These can be used in teas, cooked on their own or added to other dishes.

Preparation

Extreme care must be taken with organic produce to be sure it is free of insects. Wash thoroughly and examine carefully, especially leafy vegetables and beans. If making a lettuce salad, core lettuce, separate leaves in a sink full of water and inspect each leaf on removal for drying, as soaking alone will not remove insects. All loose-leaf vegetables, eg, spinach and silver beet, should be ßtreated in the same way. Organically grown vegetables tend to have more skin blemishes and surface dirt on them than those commercially grown with synthetic chemicals and pesticides.

Usually the skin of the vegetables is the most nutritious part, but you must ensure it is cleaned thoroughly. An essential tool for preparing organic vegetables is a firm-bristled food brush with as large a surface as you can get. It should also have a large handle on top — this makes it easier especially when preparing vegetables in bulk, eg, carrots. Place them in water and roll the brush back and forward across them to remove dirt.

The brush can also be used to remove surface blemishes from vegetables such as cauliflower — it can do this without spoiling the natural shape and texture of the florets. Brush under running water before cutting the cauliflower.

Use brush on any organic vegetables where you wish to retain the skin, eg, potatoes, celery, kumara and parsnip. Any mould or fungus remaining after brushing or cleaning should be removed before cooking, as it could become toxic when heated, especially those found on hard vegetables such as potatoes and pumpkins.

NB: Insects and dirt are practically non-existent in vegetables grown hydroponically, ie, with their roots in a water/food solution rather than soil. (See "Organic Dictionary", p.17.) They will also keep longer, especially lettuces, if kept with the root in a cup of water. (See "Keeping an Organic Kitchen — Storage", p.31-33.)

When preparing salad vegetables, cut fibrous varieties (celery, etc) across the grain to avoid stringiness. Observe all other normal preparation rules, eg, removing eyes and green parts from potatoes. Beans, especially the hard variety, should be visually inspected and then thoroughly rinsed to rid them of dirt, rocks and other foreign objects. Any hard beans, eg: kidney and chickpea, should be soaked overnight before cooking to soften the outer skin and remove any remaining dirt. Do not use the soaking water for cooking.

Frozen vegetables should be cooked, not eaten raw. Some salads mix raw and cooked ingredients, eg, eggs, potatoes and pasta. Do not mix the cooked ingredients with raw ingredients while still hot, as this can soften the raw ingredients. It is also a bacteria contamination risk, especially if adding a dressing, such as mayonnaise, which contains raw egg. Pasta, rice or any starchy substance in a salad, should be rinsed immediately after cooking to remove excess starch, which would cause them to clump together while cooling. If using sprouted vegetables, seeds or grains in salads, refer to "Sprouting", p.84-85.

NB: Organic vegetables, because they are usually locally grown, are "ripened on the vine" before sale, and therefore will have more nutritional value and natural sugar. If a recipe calls for a sweetener, you may need to reduce or even eliminate this ingredient.

Plain tofu is tasteless while tempeh has a slight flavour due to its fermentation. Both will readily absorb spices and sauces. They are common substitutes in countries where meat is seldom eaten, or where it is expensive and needs to be "stretched". Tofu and tempeh are especially convenient because they can be sliced as patties, cut into chunks or shaped into sausages, and can be marinated like meat for a desired flavour. Both can be stored for a long period of time in the refrigerator, submerged in water which must be changed at least every other day. They should last at least three weeks under this method. Other processed organic vegetables products are coming onto the market, eg, TVP (textured vegetable protein), which are usually dehydrated and highly processed and in the authors' opinion thus lacking in nutritional value. You can make your own fresh TVP alternative without all these processes and end up with something better tasting and fresher.

Cooking Methods — In Order of Preference

Vegetables are usually cooked one of two ways — soft or firm. "Soft-cooked" vegetables, eg, in roasts, stews and curries, or mashed, should not be over-cooked to the point of losing texture. Over-cooked potatoes, for instance, turn into a watery mush; even potatoes being boiled for mashing should still retain their shape and texture. If they start to flake and fall apart when draining, the potatoes are over-cooked. They should have a fluffy texture when mashed. On the other hand, "firm-cooked" vegetables, eg, stir-fried, steamed, grilled/barbecued, salad potatoes, should not be under-cooked. When stir-frying vegetables they should all be just on the point of becoming soft. Always start with the hardest vegetables, eg, carrots, then follow with broccoli or cauliflower, adding softer varieties last, eg, capsicum, zucchini, cabbage, spring onion.

When boiling potatoes for a salad, cut into the salad shape first and cook until the outside is soft but the inside still firm. Imaginative cooking makes our body's nutritional needs more enjoyable, and vegetables that are not overcooked or drenched with salt have more flavour and better texture.

Vegetables eaten as a side dish with meat can be cooked either with the meat course or separately, and can be cooked in all the methods previously mentioned. When cooking vegetables on their own, steaming is the best method to ensure they are not overcooked. Baking vegetables loose or in a pan can be done easily without using aluminium foil. Vegetables with an outer skin, such as potatoes, can be left exposed to the heat. Where there is no outer skin, eg, pumpkins and carrots, cover the pan with a lid to retain the natural juices. Use the smallest pan possible to keep the vegetables close together and prevent moisture loss.

When frying any vegetables, for instance stir-frying, avoid blanching beforehand; this is an unnecessary process that robs them of nutritional value, taste and texture. Boiling tends to do the same, but if it is needed, always bring the water to the boil before adding the vegetables, then follow "Cooking Time" instructions, p.106.

As stated before, hard beans should be soaked before cooking because cooking raw will produce a tough outer texture and a mushy interior one. Overnight soaking softens the outer skin and ensures a more even cooking process. If soaking has not been possible, place beans in water, bring to boil and cook for 5-10 minutes, then drain and cover again with cold water and proceed with normal cooking. This will remove dirt and help prevent the "tough-mushy" texture. Soft beans do not usually require soaking and require minimal cooking. Sprouted beans, whatever variety, can be eaten raw in salads or cooked.

Processed vegetable products (eg, tofu and tempeh) or sea-grown vegetables do not require a lot of cooking, which is done mainly to enhance the flavour. Seasoning and marinating should take place at least two hours before cooking to ensure the desired flavour is absorbed, otherwise the taste will only be on the outside. If using ready-made TVP products, follow instructions. If using your own TVP alternative, remember you will most likely be cooking twice, so the initial cooking should be minimal before placing in food processor.

Cooking Times

Judge your vegetables.

- If vegetables taste good raw or are not hard, eg, celery, capsicum and zucchini, they need minimum cooking time (3-10 minutes boiling or frying; 10-15 minutes baking, grilling or barbecuing).
- If vegetables are soft, eg, carrots, pumpkin and potatoes, cooking time should be increased (approximately 7-25 minutes frying or boiling; 15-40 minutes baking, grilling or barbecuing, depending on whether covered or uncovered).

NB: Some firm vegetables vary in texture within their own grouping, and so cooking time may need to be increased. Leafy and soft vegetables, such as cabbage, silverbeet, spinach, zucchini, capsicum, mushrooms and onions, usually should be added last and cooked the least, if not just heated. No leafy vegetable should be cooked for more than five minutes. For processed vegetable products, follow same instructions.

- Hard beans, after soaking, should be cooked for a minimum of two hours if boiling or baking, unless sprouted, in which case 45 minutes is sufficient.
- Soft beans need only 10-20 minutes' boiling or baking. When using beans in stir-fry, hard beans must be sprouted and both soft and hard cooked no more than 15 minutes.

Fruits and Nuts

Most fruits and nuts, if not eaten raw on their own, are generally used as an ingredient of or accompaniment to another item or dish. With fruits, there is a noticeable taste difference between organically and commercially grown products. Because fruits are mostly liquid, they retain the taste and residues of any liquid synthetic chemicals used. Organic fruits, like vegetables, are normally grown for local use rather than export, so they are usually "ripened on the vine" and therefore will be sweeter than their commercially grown counterparts.

Frozen fruits, unlike vegetables, are enjoyable either raw or cooked, and the natural acidity in most fruits makes them safe to eat when thawed without cooking.

Organic nuts differ from their commercial counterparts only in the time they will keep. Because they contain no synthetic fungicide, they are especially vulnerable to moulds and fungi. Some nut moulds can be highly toxic and if a bag of nuts is showing signs of contamination it is best to throw away the whole bag. Due to a lack of pesticides, they are also vulnerable to insects, and care should be taken in storage. (See "Keeping an Organic Kitchen — Storage", p.31-33.)

Organic fruits and nuts deliver maximum nutritional value when eaten uncooked. Like vegetables, most organic fruit and nut varieties cannot be imported into New Zealand because they will have to be sprayed with synthetic chemicals. They are therefore subject to seasonal availability. (See "How to Eat Organically All-Year-Round — Seasonal Availability & Bottling and Preserving", p.38-39, p.48.)

Preparation

Wash organic fruits thoroughly and inspect for insects. If preparing fruit in bulk with the skin on, eg, oranges and apples, place them in water and run the vegetable brush (see "Vegetables — Preparation", p.102-103) over them — this saves time. Any cutting, seeding or coring should be done before cooking.

If cooking fruit in water, use the minimum amount of water necessary. If possible, use the actual juice from the fruits rather than water, or add a complementary fruit juice, eg, apple. This method will also add sweetness, making sugar unnecessary.

Fruits can be homogenised fresh, cooked or frozen with a food processor or masticating juicer, for use with other fruits or in association with ingredients as milk, ice-cream or yoghurt. (See also "Keeping an Organic Kitchen —

Storage", p.31-33.) For instructions on preparing dried fruit, see "How to Eat Organically All-Year-Round — Bottling and Preserving", p.48.

Nuts should be inspected for foreign objects but not washed unless absolutely necessary because the water will soften the shells, making them decay more quickly and become mouldy. If they must be washed, ensure they are dried quickly and thoroughly, preferably on a towel in the sun.

Nuts should be refrigerated after cooking, or processing into butter (for satay, etc), because they are especially vulnerable to bacteria and flavour loss in this state.

Cooking Methods — In Order of Preference

Steaming is the best method for cooking fruits, followed by baking, boiling or blanching. (See also "How to Eat Organically All-Year-Round — Bottling and Preserving", p.48.) Some fruits are also suitable for eastern dishes, such as kebabs and curries.

If possible, use fresh fruits when baking. Remember, if using preserved fruits you will be cooking them twice, so they will end up with less flavour, texture and nutritional value.

Nuts are most often baked, roasted or fried, which are the preferable cooking methods. When baking or roasting, spread nuts evenly in a shallow pan. To avoid burning, they should be baked at a moderate temperature, shaking the pan occasionally, and if frying they should be roasted beforehand and then stirred frequently.

Blanching, which is used for removing shells and husks or softening of the nuts, also robs them of flavour. Buy shelled, unblanched nuts and roast with the husks on, then remove the husks by rubbing them in the palms of your hands. To get rid of the husks afterwards, take the nuts and husks outside in the roasting pan and turn a hair dryer on them to blow the husks away.

NB: Husks should be removed, as they have a bitter taste. (See also "Keeping an Organic Kitchen — Storage", p.31-33.)

Cooking Times

Fruits and nuts are generally cooked to change or enhance taste, and in the case of fruits, to achieve softness. As with all things, this is a matter of taste, but as a rule of thumb, unless using for a jam or sauce, fruits should be heated rather than cooked through to retain nutritional value and taste.

The firmer the flesh or the thicker the skin, the longer the cooking time required. It is a good ideas to taste during the cooking to judge when the fruit is ready, rather than setting an arbitrary cooking time.

With recipes such as pies, it is possible to cook the crust first and then add the fruit. When heating the fruit, keep in mind that it will be heated again when the pie is baked.

Nuts are generally cooked to achieve crispness. Cooking time will vary according to quantity and type. For example, when oven roasting nuts, stir them regularly, checking frequently, until the desired taste and texture are achieved. The basic rule to follow is: The harder and/or bigger the nut, the longer the cooking time. As with fruits, tasting the nuts during cooking will help you achieve the flavour and texture desired.

NB: *If using nuts for a baking recipe, the cooking time should be taken into account when roasting.*

Meal Makers and Complements

Grains

Rice and millet are two of the most common organic grains and can be used in similar ways, either as the basis of a main course or as a side dish. It should be noted here that organic "white" rice is not readily available because the "whitening" process actually involves removing the outer husk and polishing the grain. This is generally believed to reduce the rice's nutritional value.

The same principle applies to millet, although its outer shell flakes easily and is of lesser value. All "whole" grains can contain foreign objects and should be inspected visually before cooking.

Preparation

If a special flavour is desired, eg, onions, garlic or spices, these should be sautéd together and the grain and water added to them.

NB: *Any salt should be added to the grain before the water, to ensure a better mixture.*

Cooking Methods — In Order of Preference

Whatever the desired final result, whole grains should always be boiled. However, the key to the flavour of the grain lies in when the boiling takes place. For instance, the Chinese boil their rice with little or no spices before stir-frying it, adding the main spices during the latter process. Spanish-style rice is fried first, with all the spices and other ingredients, followed by the salt and water. The dish is then covered and boiled. When stir-frying in both cases, the rice should be constantly stirred to avoid burning. Note that millet can be used as a substitute for rice in such dishes.

When using more than four cups of grain, ensure water covers to the depth of approximately one inch. If using whole grains for baking, they must be boiled beforehand, and any seasoning added during boiling.

Cooking Times

All grains should be boiled for 25-30 minutes. If cooking a second time, eg, stir-frying or baking, take the boiling time into account. The second cooking is only for the benefit of the other ingredients. If the grain is being used hot from boiling, it will require half the cooking time of grain that has been allowed to cool.

Pasta and Noodles

Noodles were developed very early on in the history of the human diet. They were invented by the Chinese around 5,000 BC, but the first European to taste them was Marco Polo, in the 13th century. This Italian started a food revolution in his home country, which turned the noodles into pasta.

There is a wide variety of organic pasta available, fresh and dehydrated, including durum wheat, vegetable, wheat-free, macrobiotic and brown rice. Noodles are also available in these varieties.

Durum, a hard wheat, is grown in New Zealand and Australia. It is ground, mixed with water, kneaded, shaped and dried to make pasta, as is rice flour. Herbs, spices, vegetables and other natural ingredients can be added during this process.

Making pasta is a complex process and you will need a specialist instruction book for this if you insist on your organic pasta being really fresh! Organic ingredients will react basically the same as commercial products, so just follow the instructions but remember it will have a much shorter shelf life and should be used as soon as possible.

Cooking Methods

Whatever you are going to do with your pasta or noodles, the first thing you will do is boil them. Remember not to contaminate them with tap water! And be sure to use enough water — use too little and starch will coagulate on the surface of the water, affecting the quality of what you are cooking. Use a large pot for boiling pasta or noodles, and make sure the depth of water on top is well past the second joint of your index finger. Use salt at your own discretion and be sure to add before the water is boiling. Stir during boiling to ensure even cooking.

If added to a salad, pasta should always be rinsed in cold water to prevent sticking, and mixed with other salad ingredients before placing in the refrigerator. Handle lasagne sheets the same way before baking. When eating boiled pasta, such as spaghetti, hot, the pasta should be the last item cooked, and it should be served immediately. A sprinkle of organic oil, eg, olive, after draining will help prevent sticking. You can also add fresh herbs, such as basil, to the pasta at this point.

The rule about cooking last also applies to noodles. You can add flavour ingredients, meat, vegetables or broth to the noodles while boiling. If using noodles in a stir-fry, add last to avoid burning.

Cooking Times

These will depend on whether you require your pasta firm or soft, and the amount you are cooking. The only way to be sure your pasta is properly cooked is to taste it. Bite through a piece. If pasta is to be baked in a dish such as macaroni or lasagne afterwards, consider the boiling time as part of the overall cooking time. Dishes like macaroni cheese should be cooked mostly in the middle of the oven, and then moved under the grill for the last few minutes, to brown the top. Noodles usually require less boiling than pasta, but the same rules apply. If adding to a stir-fry, do not boil the noodles for too long, as they continue to cook when frying. Organic pasta and noodles tend to cook faster by up to several minutes than their commercial counterparts, and fresh pasta always cooks faster than dehydrated.

Eggs and Dairy Products

While eggs are often eaten on their own, especially at breakfast time, both eggs and dairy products are used mainly as ingredients of recipes. Organic eggs are from free-ranged chickens, but eggs labelled "Free- Range" are not necessarily organic. (See "Organic Dictionary".) Organic eggs are more gluti-nous because of their higher protein content. This is beneficial in baking and sauces where thickness and texture are important.

In some recipes you will be able to use fewer eggs, if you prefer, and where the recipe calls for separating the yolk and the white for thickness, you may be able to use more of the yolk for extra nutritional value without compromising texture.

In New Zealand the access to raw dairy products is strictly-controlled and they are not readily available at time of writing, even though they have an indisputably higher nutritional value than those which have been processed, eg, pasteurised. However, organic pasteurised milk is readily obtainable at this time, in the North Island at least.

Pasteurisation was named after the 19th century French scientist Louis Pasteur, who discovered that milk products would not retain various troublesome germs if heated almost to boiling point. This was a revolutionary concept which saved many lives at a time of no refrigeration.

However, the process also destroys vitamins and reduces minerals and other beneficial contents of milk. The threat of listeria and tuberculosis has been used as a reason for pasteurising dairy products, but it should be remembered that the listeria bacteria that are naturally present in raw milk in a small quantity are being used to fight certain cancers. And the theory that tuberculosis can be transmitted from cows to humans through their milk is currently being discredited — in fact it is now clear that some strains of tuberculosis emerging have nothing to do with raw milk and are resistant to present antibiotics!

Some researchers even claim the antibiotics used in the raising of food products have helped in the development of these "super strains". All this just adds fuel to the argument in favour of the organic diet. Raw organic milk, if available, will have half the shelf life of its pasteurised counterpart, but if heated for cooking it will undergo a de-facto "pasteurisation", which will increase its shelf life to the same level and not affect the shelf life of the product in which it is used. When using any milk that is not homogenised, remember the fat and liquid will separate, affecting recipes such as ice-cream. Running milk through a masticating juicer (see "Keeping an Organic Kitchen", p.30) will remedy this.

Most organic dairy products, including a wide variety of cheeses and yoghurts, are available in New Zealand. These are usually made from homogenised or pasteurised milk, but some raw organic milk products are also available. Raw organic dairy products will tend to have a stronger taste and shorter shelf life than their commercial counterparts. Cheese made from raw milk will have a higher fat content, so use less cooking oil or fat in hot dishes.

Cooking Methods

Raw milk products will curdle more easily during cooking, so if adding to a dish, either allow the mixture to go off the boil first (in sauces, stews or curries), or stir constantly when heating, at a low temperature. Bring slowly up to desired heat.

Raw Foods

It is a fact that most foods lose some nutritional value when cooked. As we have stated before, organic products are higher in nutritional value and will deliver their best with minimum cooking. Cooking certainly enhances flavour, but for maximum nutritional benefit, raw is definitely a viable alternative for people who enjoy that natural flavour.

When most people think of raw food, they think of salads or seafood, but there are many dishes commonly eaten cooked which also can be served uncooked. A well-known "raw" dish is gazpacho soup, but even though it is served cold, some recipes call for a bouillon cube or stock, which will have been cooked beforehand. For a raw alternative bouillon, mince or crush onion, celery, carrot, potato, garlic, basil, oregano and salt, and mix together. The last three spices are optional, and the amount of carrot and potato used should be about half the proportions of onion and celery. Judge the quantity of bouillon needed for yourself, but you start by using less in a raw dish.

Because there is no cooking process involved, you can be more flexible and add more of one ingredient if you feel it's necessary later on. You may also need to add other ingredients, eg, chillies, ginger, parsley or mint, to compensate for the lack of cooking flavour. A simple example of changing a cooked recipe to a raw one is tomato soup, which uses the same ingredients but changes the process.

TOMATO SOUP

Ingredients

750 g tomatoes	30 g butter
1 medium onion, finely chopped	1 carrot, finely chopped
3/4 cup vegetable stock	1/2 tsp basil
1/4 tsp ground pepper	1 tsp salt
1 tblsp honey	1/4 cup cream

Method

These are the ingredients for a cooked organic tomato soup. To prepare them raw, you will need a food processor and preferably a masticating juicer. Assuming you have already made your raw vegetable stock, as shown opposite, you will then need to juice the tomatoes. This will give you less juice than you would get if you cooked the tomatoes, so you will need more — about a kilo.

Prepare other ingredients, combine with the juiced tomatoes in the food processor and mix to soup consistency.

Some tomato soup recipes call for flour or cornflour as a thickener, but this would not taste good in a raw soup. Instead, try nuts which have been soaked at least overnight or sprouted, (see "Sprouting", p.84-85), and then finely minced. Try a single ice cube for a garnish if serving in hot weather.

Nuts and grains usually need some form of processing, and in raw dishes, soaking is the alternative to roasting or other cooking methods. They are then crushed, chopped or minced for use in the final recipe, where a flour or grain is called for.

Here are some further examples of cooked meals that can be converted to serve raw.

CREAM OF CARROT

Ingredients

10 medium carrots

1/2 medium onion

1 cup cream (optional)

5 garlic cloves

1/4 cup soaked or sprouted
nuts (eg, walnuts or pistachio)

1/2 tsp nutmeg

1 tsp oregano

Method

Juice carrots, retaining juice and pulp separately. Place juice in food processor, add crushed garlic and oregano, chopped onion and other ingredients except carrot pulp.

Process well, then start adding carrot pulp to thicken the mixture. This is a substitute for the cream if a non-dairy dish is preferred, or some of the pulp can be used in addition with the cream. Garnish with parsley. Can be served on its own or as a dip with sliced vegetables.

NUT LOAF

Ingredients

1 tsp oregano

5 garlic cloves

$1/2$ medium onion

4 carrots

$1/4$ cup fresh parsley

1 tsp curry powder (optional)

2 tblsp tahini

3 spring onions

1 cup raw bouillon

$1/4$ cup pumpkin
  and/or sunflower seeds

$1/4$ cup each soaked almonds,
  cashews and pecans (other varieties
  can be substituted)

Method

Crush oregano and garlic, chop onions and carrots, add with other ingredients, except nuts and seeds, to food processor, mix well, then add nuts and seeds, mix all together, then turn food processor on again, switching on and off until a mealy consistency is achieved.

Place in a loaf dish, cover with desired sauce and serve.

FROZEN FRUIT PIE

Pie Base Ingredients

$1/2$ cup soaked nuts
(any type may be used)

1 tblsp honey

$1/3$ cup soaked oats

$1/3$ cup soaked bran

Filling Ingredients

2 bananas

1 cup strawberries

1 cup raspberries,

1 tsp honey

Method

Peel bananas, slice if desired, and freeze all fruit ingredients together overnight.
To make pie base, put all base ingredients in the food processor and grind to a mealy texture, adding a little water to the mixture if required. Remove mixture from processor and flatten into a pie dish. Do not add filling until just before serving.

When ready to serve, place frozen fruit and honey into food processor and blend until an almost creamy texture is achieved. If desired, add a liqueur or other alcohol, eg, cherry brandy, for a more exotic taste.

Pour into the pie base, garnish with fresh slices of fruit and serve immediately.

RAW APPLE PIE

Pie Base Ingredients

1 cup soaked walnuts or almonds
1 cup seedless dates

3/4 cup raisins

Filling Ingredients

4-5 apples
Cinnamon, nutmeg and cloves
(1/2 tsp each or to taste)

1 tsp vanilla extract
Juice of 1 lemon
1 tsp honey (optional)

Method

Soak walnuts or almonds at least overnight, or sprout (see "Sprouting", p.84-85).

Place in food processor and grind to a meal, then mix in a bowl with remaining pie base ingredients and press into a pie dish to form the crust.

Peel and core apples, place in food processor with all other filling ingredients and process to a chunky texture by turning processor on and off. Pour into crust and serve.

Desserts

Desserts are often perceived as having more aesthetic than nutritional value, but when they are made with organic ingredients they give you the best of both worlds. You will need to be adaptable in your choice of desserts because of the seasonal availability of organic ingredients, such as fruit. Balance is also important when choosing a dessert — if you have served a substantial main course, there probably will not be room for a pie or pudding afterwards, so something lighter is more appropriate for dessert, and vice versa with a lighter main course. Desserts are often colourful affairs, but this effect is usually achieved through artificial ingredients. A colourful organic dessert may require a more imaginative mix of ingredients, eg, more varieties of fruit.

A large variety of organic dairy products is available around the country, with the glaring exception of ice-cream. Little is available at the time of writing and therefore you will probably need to make your own. An ice-cream recipe can be found in the "Recipes" section, p.170.

A food processor is a must for making organic desserts, and a blender is also useful. Most of the organic yoghurts (acidophilus, Bulgarian, etc) are available only in plain form, allowing you to use fresh or frozen organic fruits to create your own flavours. And if you want to homogenise the flavour, you will need a masticating juicer.

For baked desserts, all varieties and grades of flour, including pastry, are available in organic form. Remember that organic flour is freshly-ground and contains no synthetic chemicals, so it should be kept in the refrigerator if storing for any length of time. Also, the lack of conditioning agents affects the raising qualities. (For more information, see "Baking", p.129.) Baked desserts are generally better if the texture is softer, so it is preferable if using a harder flour to mix it with lighter grain or white flour.

To most of us, sweetness is the essence of a dessert and it should not be regarded negatively, especially when considering the organic possibilities! Remember first, when selecting dessert ingredients, that organically grown fruits and vegetables are normally picked when fully ripe. They will therefore contain more natural sugar than their commercial counterparts, which are ripened after picking. You can use this difference to your advantage, as you will need less or no added sweetener, a special plus for diabetics.

As stated elsewhere, sugar is not currently available in organic form and to our knowledge no alternative sweetener is available as a dry ingredient. If it is, it has probably been highly processed, eg, dehydrated, and so its nutritional value will be low. Liquid alternatives are available, eg, honey, maple syrup and fruit extracts. For more information about sweeteners and their uses, see "Organic Cooking"' p.66-67.

A general tip is to use fruit extracts as sweeteners in any dessert where the main ingredient is fruit, and to use honey or maple syrup in baking. For icings, a dark recipe can be made using organic cocoa or carob powder mixed with a bland honey and vanilla extract. White icing is not possible to make organically because organic caster and icing sugar are not available. You will have to substitute with a "glaze" mixture of honey and vanilla extract. The same substitutes will also have to be made in baking ingredients.

Unfortunately, organic cream cannot be whipped because it has not been subjected to commercial processes. You will have to substitute with ice-cream or use it plain — whipping only thickens it slightly. Honey or another sweetener can be added, then give it a few minutes in the blender. You should get an acceptable substitute.

At the time of writing, wine and beer are the only alcohol available in organic form, so be aware of this if your dessert recipe calls for any alcohol ingredient. When buying spirits or liqueurs, check the labels carefully for chemicals, especially colourings, flavourings, and preservatives. Cheaper brands tend to use more artificial ingredients.

As outlined at the start of this section, the type of dessert should be determined by what has gone before. If you have served a spicy, exotic main course, people might welcome something light, cool and refreshing for dessert. People who have been served an entirely cooked main course, eg, a roast dinner, might especially enjoy a raw dessert. Organic fruits and vegetables are especially good raw because they have not been drenched with synthetic chemicals and are higher in nutritional value. Fruit salad is an obvious example, but in the "Raw Foods" section, p.114-117, you will find ideas for such desserts as raw apple pie. The main point to remember when selecting a dessert is that it's the taste people remember easiest, because it came last. Make it memorable!

Breakfasts and Baby Foods

Whether starting your day or starting in life, organic food is undoubtedly the best start of all. Organic breakfast foods are slowly becoming available commercially but the variety is limited at present. However, the baby food situation is much better, driven by consumer concern for infant health, especially in regards to food allergies and the effects of pesticides and other synthetic chemicals.

The Organic Breakfast

While ready-prepared organic breakfast foods are still scarce, you can buy individual ingredients to prepare your own. Organic eggs, bacon and bread are all readily available, as are sausages and all other breakfast meats. Organic fruit availability is governed by the seasons, but a suitable breakfast fruit is usually available fresh at any time of the year. The same applies to fruit juices.

Pancakes are another breakfast favourite and organic maple syrup is widely available, but fruit toppings will have to be made. Most pancake recipes can be easily converted to include all organic ingredients, but if using a heavier flour, such as wholemeal, you should make the mixture a little runnier than normal, otherwise the pancakes might not cook properly. Pancakes make an excellent hot dessert on a cold night, with cream and fresh fruit, or they can be eaten cold as a snack, in small pikelets. Pancakes can also be made more nutritional by adding ground seeds or nuts which have been soaked overnight.

Cereal is the most common breakfast food these days, with an increasing number of people wanting a low-fat, high-fibre start. Whatever cereal you choose, milk and/or cream will be the most common ingredient. These are readily available in organic form, as are soy milk and vegetable and grain-derived milk alternatives for dairy-free diets.

If you want to make your own cereal, you will be able to choose from a wide variety of organic grains. These are often roasted in cereals, such as muesli.

If you want porridge, you can get prepared rolled oats in organic form from most shops. But if you buy the oats fresh yourself and want to roll them, you should spread them out on a wooden cutting board and smash them with a rolling pin. By breaking down the hull in this manner, you expose more of the surface to be cooked. Sometimes, slightly roasting them beforehand makes the process easier and increases flavour. You can cook your porridge using milk or water according to taste. Oats have a mild natural sweetness, so you can be sparing in adding other sweeteners.

A simple recipe is to boil 1 cup of rolled oats in 2 1/2 cups of water with 1 tsp of salt. Once boiling, reduce heat and simmer covered for 20 minutes. Serve with milk, cream or honey if desired.

Muesli is also easy to make and the only limit to the ingredients is your imagination. The most common base grain, again, is rolled oats.

ORGANIC MUSELI

Basic Ingredients

5 cups rolled oats

1 cup toasted wheatgerm

1 tsp salt

1/2 cup sunflower seeds

1/2 cup chopped nuts of your choice

1 cup bran

1/2 cup honey

1 cup raisins

Butter or vegetable oil

Method

You need a large shallow oven dish, greased with either butter or oil.

Place the oats, wheatgerm, bran, nuts and seeds (if raw) in the dish. Bake in a pre-heated oven at 180°C for 20-25 minutes, stirring constantly to avoid burning. The oats should be light brown and crisp.

Add honey and stir through the mixture, return to the oven and roast for another 5 minutes, still stirring. If the oats appear too dry, add a little water (1/4 cup maximum) during the last 5 minutes.

Allow to cool and add the raisins. Place in an airtight, preferably glass container, until needed.

Finish off your organic breakfast with tea or coffee, many varieties of both being available in organic form, along with herbal teas and coffee alternatives.

Baby Food

For convenience sake, organic baby food is now widely available, but you may prefer to prepare it yourself to gain maximum nutritional value from organic produce. Commercially produced baby food will have been cooked at least once during the bottling or canning process. Therefore, reheating will further reduce the nutritional value.

Naturally, baby food has to taste good as well as being nutritious. The best combination comes from using sweet vegetables as a base (carrots, kumara, buttercup, etc), and then a medium-taste vegetable (potatoes, zucchini, cauliflower, etc) as the main ingredient, and finally topping it off with the stronger-tasting vegetables (broccoli, peas, beans, etc). This provides a nutritionally balanced and tasty meal.

Here are some baby food recipe ideas that are quick and easy to prepare.

Baby Food Recipes

The following information applies to all the recipes listed below.

Prep time: 5-10 minutes
Number of servings: 4
Shelf life: Refrigerate for up to 3 days
Utensils: Food processor or mixer (bowl and masher if you don't have either appliance), stainless steel pot for boiling.

BROCCOLI SURPRISE

Cooking time: 8 minutes

Ingredients

1 medium potato   *1/2 cup carrots**

*1/4 cup broccoli**   *Purified water*

Method

Peel and dice potato and carrots, place in boiling water (use minimum amount needed) and cover. Meanwhile cut broccoli flowers. When potato and carrots are just soft (usually after 5 minutes), add broccoli, cover and cook for 3 more minutes. Drain and place in food processor, mixer or bowl, then homogenise or mash as finely as possible. Serve.

Cook's Tips

You may want to experiment with the cooking time for the potato and carrots, or perhaps add the carrots a minute or two later.

* See chart on "Seasonal Availability."

PUMPKIN EATER

Cooking time: 15 minutes

Ingredients

1 cup pumpkin*
(buttercup preferably)
1/4 cup broccoli*

1 small-medium potato
1/4 cup cauliflower*
Purified water

Method

Chop pumpkin into small cubes, place in boiling water and cover. Meanwhile, peel and dice potato, chop cauliflower and broccoli. After 7 minutes, add potato, cover and simmer another 5 minutes, then add cauliflower and broccoli, cover again and simmer another 3 minutes. Drain, process or mash and serve.

Cook's Tips

The time for cooking the pumpkin may be shorter depending on the type of pumpkin used — the flesh is harder in some than in others.

KUMARA KAI

Cooking time: 8 minutes

Ingredients

1 cup kumara*
1/2 cup carrot*

1 cup cauliflower*

Method

Peel and dice kumara and carrot, place in boiling water, cover and simmer for 5 minutes, then add cauliflower, cover again and leave another three minutes. Drain, process or mash and serve.

Cooking time: 15 minutes

Ingredients

*1 cup kumara**

*¹/₄ cup peas**

Purified water

*¹/₂ cup pumpkin**

*¹/₈ cup zucchini**

Method

Peel and dice kumara and pumpkin, place pumpkin into boiling water and cover. Meanwhile peel and slice zucchini, shell peas (if necessary).

Add kumara to pumpkin after 7 minutes, cover and simmer for another 5 minutes, then add peas and zucchini, cover and cook a further 3 minutes. Drain, process or mash and serve.

Organic & Dietary Tips

These recipes are free of all animal products, wheat, cooking oils, sweeteners, spices, seasonings and added salt. This means there is less risk of developing food allergies. They are easily digested and are a good step towards introducing children to solid food.
*See Chart on "Seasonal Availability".

Baking

As explained in the introduction to this section (see "Organic Cooking", p.65-69), you will need to learn, or re-learn, traditional baking methods in order to produce baked organic food. Organic grains, flours and non-wheat flours are easily obtained. (See "Product Availability", p.40-41). Raising agents, such as yeast and soda bicarbonate, are generally assumed to be organic although they are not currently certifiable as such. Your best advice, to avoid any artificial additives, would be to purchase these ingredients through health shops.

Yeast is the traditional raising agent, producing gases which cause the dough to rise. It is available in dried form for convenience, but fresh is preferable. Fresh yeast should not be kept any longer than five days in a cool place, or two weeks in a refrigerator. Dried yeast is more concentrated, so you need only a third or half as much as you would if using fresh yeast.

Because free-range and organic eggs (see "Product Availability", p.47) have a higher protein content than their battery-reared counterparts, mixing them with organic flour will help substitute for conditioners used in commercial flours. They will also enhance texture and richness of baked dishes.

Butter and oil are the only fats used in the baking recipes in this book. Cooking oil can be substituted for butter, for those who do not eat animal products, but it will not give the same flavour or texture. Use less oil than butter. A useful guide to using liquid in a recipe is 300 ml of fluid to 450 g of standard wholemeal flour. The softer the flour, the less liquid is necessary.

In most recipes you should add all the liquid at once. It is easier to add more flour if the mixture is too sticky, than to add more liquid to a dry flour mix. When using warm liquid with flour, it should be between 38 and 43ºC. Sea salt adds flavour to yeast mixtures and prevents the yeast from fermenting too quickly.

NB: *Too much salt will kill the yeast and the omission of salt will result in a sticky, rather than elastic texture. Thus, if eliminating salt for dietary reasons, you will end up with a heavier product. All the baking recipes in this book use honey rather than sugar, which is not available in organic form.*

Preparation

If you desire to use a sprouted product in baking, you must create it before preparing dough. (See "Organic Cooking — Sprouting", p.84-85). For baking purposes, you are sprouting for the root only.

Mix sprouted product with flour before preparing dough for raising. Because sprouted oats add volume, reduce slightly the amount of flour called for in the recipe, judging the amount by the texture of the dough. (It should have same texture as without sprouted ingredients.) When using larger sprouting material, eg, lentils, you may want to chop briefly in a blender before adding to flour.

Using the above instructions you can combine different sprouted products in your favourite recipes or in those given in this book. Raw sprouted ingredients have a higher protein content and therefore add nutritional value to the finished product, although a little of the benefit will be lost during baking. Sprouted ingredients can be used in many combinations to produce more exotic breads. They are a nutritional and flavour enhancer, and are usually added to traditional baking recipes. For these reasons we have not included specific sprouted recipes — variations can be made on the recipes in this book.

NB: Water used for sprouting should be changed if process takes longer than two days, such as with seeds. Most raising agents carry instructions, but if you are using yeast, you should learn the traditional ways of preparing dough, outlined below.

1. Basic Method

- With fresh yeast, mix first with liquid ingredients before adding to flour.
- For a quick rise, the liquids should be warmed to 38-43°C.
- With dry yeast, dissolve a teaspoon of honey, or preferred sweetener, in warm liquid ingredients, sprinkle in yeast and leave in a warm place for 10 minutes until frothy, then add to remaining ingredients.

2. Rubbing Method

This is the easiest method, but is only suitable for fresh yeast.

- Rub the yeast into the flour, breaking it up if necessary.
- Add liquid and make a soft dough.
- Beat with your hand, a wooden spoon or fork to distribute the yeast evenly.

3. Batter Method

This is especially useful for rich mixtures using lots of honey, butter and egg. In such doughs, the growth of the yeast is retarded and this can be overcome by forming a batter.

- Use one-third of the flour from the recipe, all of the yeast (fresh or dry) all the liquid (warmed) and some of the honey (1 teaspoon maximum).
- No salt should be added, as it slows down the yeast.
- Mix batter, cover and let stand in warm place for 20 minutes, if using fresh yeast, and 30 minutes, if dry.
- Add the rest of the flour and all other ingredients, eg, eggs, fruit, nuts, etc, and mix to a dough.

Mixing

Mixing can be done by hand or by a mechanical mixer with a dough-hook attachment. If using a mixer, follow the instruction book. If mixing by hand, add all liquids to dry ingredients in a large bowl and mix with hands, spoon or fork until dough no longer clings to bowl.

When using butter, it should be rubbed into the dry flour before adding the liquids. (Use the heel of your hand inside the bowl — and let the butter soften at room temperature before using.) Add extra flour if dough is too sticky to handle.

Kneading

Kneading must take place after mixing to ensure a good rise and even texture. This can be done mechanically (follow instructions) or by hand. To knead dough manually:

- Place dough on flat surface, eg, a table or wooden cutting board lightly dusted with flour.
- Form dough into one large round ball; fold towards you, then push in opposite direction with heel of your hand.
- Repeat this process for about 8 minutes or until the dough is smooth and elastic in texture. During this process you may need to sprinkle on more flour to prevent dough from sticking to board or hands.

Raising

Raising needs to occur at least three times before baking an organic product, as opposed to the once or twice that is normal with commercial flour. This is to ensure a lighter and more even texture.

- The dough must be covered during the raising period to prevent hardening of the outside skin and loss of heat.
- Unshaped dough can be left to rise in the mixing bowl, covered with a plastic bag, or placed inside a bag that has been lightly oiled.
- Leave in a warm place (not above 38°C) for 35-45 minutes.

NB: If using only yeast as a raising agent, too much heat will kill it and cold will cause the yeast to act much more slowly; it is therefore important that the temperature in the raising area should be at least 25°C. (Some of your recipes may call for a "slow rise", using cooler conditions. In this case, follow those instructions.)

- Knocking back must be done after each raising, to remove air bubbles. To do this, remove dough from bowl, place on working surface and flatten with your knuckles.
- Repeat the kneading process, as stated before.
- Return the dough to raising bowl for another 35-45 minutes.
- Repeat knocking back and kneading, then shape in appropriate form (in an oiled loaf tin or bun tray).

NB: Ordinary dough should have almost doubled in volume by now, but organic flour, with natural raising agents, will only increase by about two-thirds. If the dough volume does not look right, you may want to raise it a third time before shaping. You will probably have to experiment to your own satisfaction, depending on the recipe.

- After shaping in the baking tins, the final raising process, called proving, is done. Leave shaped dough, in baking tins, either in a plastic bag with plenty of room for rising, or simply covered with a bag or damp cloth to prevent a crust forming.
- The final proving process should take no more than 20 minutes at the same raising temperature. The dough should be doubled in volume.
- Before placing in oven, dust with flour or add seeds (sesame, poppy, etc), or brush with milk, egg or liquid honey.

Baking

Temperature is crucial, so always pre-heat the oven to the required baking temperature before putting the mixture in. An oven thermometer may be a useful tool to have, since oven thermostats are not reliable. Do not leave oven door open any longer than necessary, to avoid temperature loss.

The position in the oven during baking is important — bake too close to the top of the oven and the top of the mixture will burn; vice versa if too close to the bottom, from where most ovens generate their heat. Loaves should be cooked in centre of the oven, and rolls nearer the top.

To prevent the top of the item from burning, place an oven tray over the topmost rack in the oven. This is especially useful in electric ovens, where excessive heat in the top of the oven can be a problem. For this reason, gas is better for baking than electricity, because it enables heat to circulate better.

Cooking times may vary from your original non-organic recipe if you are using only organic ingredients. Because you are using natural raising agents, not conditioning agents, you may want to bake at a slightly lower temperature for a slightly longer time. You will have to acquire knowledge through experience here.

The same rule applies where sugar has been replaced by a liquid sweetener, such as honey, to compensate for added moisture. A reasonable guideline is to reduce oven temperature 5-8% and increase cooking time by the same amount. A long toothpick or skewer should be used to test whether bread is cooked.

Do not open oven during baking, especially with bread loaves; a sudden gust of cold air can upset the slight rising process that occurs in the oven, known as "oven spring".

CHAPTER FIVE

The Organic Cookbook

A practical lesson in cookery, Auckland Technical School, April 1903

130

This book has been written as a practical guide to organic food, and the same can be said for the recipes section that follows. Many different cooking styles are included, from recipes tried and approved by the authors, to variations on old favourites. We have not, however, tried to fill the book with recipes. Instead we have concentrated on recipes where organic ingredients may react differently, so we can explain the different methods required in preparation.

The aim of this section is not only to give you some new tastes to try, but to explain how dishes can be adapted to organic ingredients.

All measurements, preparation instructions and times stated in these recipes are specifically-designed for organic ingredients and should be followed carefully. The cooking times are kept to a minimum so that the food retains as much nutritional value as possible. The "Cook's Tips" section advises on flavour and ingredient variations, as well as preparation techniques, storage and serving ideas. There are also organic and dietary tips, which explain product availability, seasonal fluctuations and dietary concerns.

Even if you are not planning to use some of these recipes, we suggest you read them through for their general information on organic cooking.

Baking Recipes

The following are basic dough recipes which you can use to make your favourite bread varieties by just adding the extra necessary ingredients (cheese, fruit, nuts, spices, etc) to one of these doughs.

WHITE BREAD DOUGH

Prep time: See instructions on dough preparation, p.125-126
Cooking time: 15-35 minutes (see below)
Number of servings: Depends on baking tin size (recipe yields one kilo of dough)
Shelf life: 5 days in refrigerator; otherwise 3
Utensils: Mixing bowl, loaf tins or flat tray (for buns)

Ingredients

Yeast (15 g fresh; 2 tsp dry)
400 ml milk or purified water
1 tbsp salt

2/3 tsp honey
675 g white flour
10 g butter

Method

Choose one of the methods of yeast preparation outlined earlier, and then follow mixing, dough-raising and kneading instructions. If using butter, rub into the flour before mixing. Because organic white flour is very light, you will probably only need two raisings.

After the final knocking-back and kneading, lightly oil or grease baking tin or tray, then place dough in loaf tin or divide up into buns and place on tray. Lightly dust top(s) with flour or seeds, or brush with a small amount of egg or honey. Cover and prove (see dough instructions, p.126) for final raising.

Bake in oven heated to 230°C for 15-20 minutes (buns) or 30-35 minutes (bread).
NB: *A one-kilo loaf should be baked for about 40 minutes.*

Cook's Tips

For variations on this recipe, other ingredients (fruit, nuts, etc) should be added after the dough mixing process. For a medium-light texture, use a 50-50 mixture of milk and water.

Organic & Dietary Tips

Substitute water for milk as stated above, and 10 ml oil for butter if wanting non-dairy bread. Salt can be reduced but we recommend not to eliminate it entirely.

WHOLEMEAL DOUGH

Prep time: See instructions on dough preparation, p.125-126
Cooking time: 15-40 minutes (see below)
Number of servings: Depends on baking tin size (recipe yields one kilo of dough)
Shelf life: 5 days in refrigerator; otherwise 3
Utensils: Mixing bowl, loaf tins or flat tray (for buns)

Ingredients

Yeast (25 g fresh or 3 tsp dry)
1 tbsp honey
1 tbsp salt
15 g butter

400 ml water or milk
675 g zintrofen or fine wheat
flour (AKA bread or pastry flour)

Method

Choose one of the methods of yeast preparation outlined earlier (in "Baking",
p.124-126), and then follow mixing, dough-raising and kneading instructions. If using
butter, rub into the flour before mixing.

After the final knocking-back and kneading, lightly oil or grease baking tin or
tray, then place dough in loaf tin or divide up into buns and place on tray. Lightly
dust top(s) with flour or seeds, or brush with a little egg or honey. Cover and prove
(see dough instructions, p.127-128) for final raising.

Bake in oven heated to 230°C for 18-22 minutes (buns) or 33-40 minutes (bread).

Cook's Tips

*For variations on this recipe, other ingredients (fruit, nuts, etc) should be added after
the dough mixing process. To make this bread more similar to the commercial
product, use a mixture of 2/3 white flour to 1/3 wheat. For a medium-light texture, use
a 50-50 mixture of milk and water.*

Organic & Dietary Tips

*This is a "heavy" wheat bread recipe. The flours stated above are preferable, but if
you prefer stone-ground or buckwheat flour or something similar, you will find it has
a heavier, moist texture. Substitute water for milk as stated above, and 13 ml of oil for
butter if wanting non-dairy bread. Salt can be reduced but we recommend not to
eliminate it entirely.*

SOURDOUGH BREAD

Prep time: See instructions on dough preparation, p.125-126, and Sourdough Starter (below)

Cooking time: 1 hour

Number of servings: Depends on use (makes two loaves)

Shelf life: 5 days in refrigerator; otherwise 3

Utensils: Mixing bowl, large storage jar, loaf tin

Ingredients

1 cup Sourdough Starter
    (see below)
1 cup milk
675 g white or wheat flour
    (pastry, bread flour or zintrofen)

1/2 cup honey
1/2 tsp natural raising agent
1/2 cup oil
1 1/2 tsp salt

Sourdough starter

1 tbsp active dry yeast
2 cups wholegrain flour (white, wheat or rye)

2 cups purified lukewarm water

Method

For Sourdough Starter: Dissolve yeast in water, add flour and stir thoroughly. Place in a jar and close, keeping at room temperature for three days. Starter is intended to be renewed, like a ginger beer plant. Keep one cup in a jar, stored in a cool place, renewing with added flour and water if retained longer than a week. Use the rest for a bread recipe. When starter is to be used again, add 2 cups water and 2 cups flour to jar and leave at room temperature for 8-24 hours.

For Sourdough: Stir together Starter, milk and 2 cups of the flour in a large bowl. Cover with a cloth and leave overnight. The next day, stir in honey, raising agent, salt and oil and rest of flour to make a stiff dough which can be kneaded. Allow to rise once, then knock back and prove (final raising) in baking tin. Cover and leave in warm place for 1 1/2 hours. Bake at 180°C for 1 hour.

Cook's Tips

Sourdough bread is known for its soft texture, so a soft flour, as mentioned above, is preferable.

Organic & Dietary Tips

Not suitable for non-dairy diets.

BARLEY BREAD

Prep time: See instructions on dough preparation, p.125-126
Cooking time: 45 minutes
Number of servings: Depends on use (makes two loaves)
Shelf life: 5 days in refrigerator; otherwise 3
Utensils: Mixing bowl, tray for loaf or buns

Ingredients

Yeast (25 g fresh or 3 tsp dry)

2 tbsp oil

1/4 cup purified water

1 tsp salt

1/4 cup honey

1 3/4 cups milk

1 kg barley flour

Method

Use basic dough preparation method No1, p.126, for fresh or dry yeast, then follow mixing and kneading instructions. Two raisings should be adequate. Dough will rise very slightly but will not double. After first raising process, knock back and re-knead, then form into a (preferably) round loaf or individual buns.

Place on an oiled or greased baking tray, cover with wet towel and let rise for 1 hour. Place in oven heated to 220°C and bake for 45-60 minutes, (depending on your oven because of heaviness of barley flour).

Cook's Tips

The above recipe has a distinctive and possibly acquired taste. An alternative flour mix of 500 g barley, 250 g wholewheat flour and 250 g white flour will give you a lighter texture and milder taste.

For a distinct barley flavour in this mixture, lightly toast the barley in the oven before mixing. For a nut bread variation, add two eggs during mixing of flour (use alternative mix), then add nuts to finished dough.

Organic & Dietary Tips

For non-dairy diets, milk can be eliminated and water substituted, but this will produce a flaky loaf. Soy milk could be used instead, but the result will be similar. Salt should not be reduced as this will adversely affect dough texture.

BRAN BREAD

Bran is actually part of the wheat kernel, and is usually added to bread, not baked on its own. Traditionally it is used in the Wholemeal Dough recipe, p.133, but can be made with any of the other bread recipes here. Simply add 100 g of bran and follow other instructions.

Cook's Tips

Since bran is is similar to wholemeal, you may want to use the commercial wholemeal bread recipe (see "Cook's Tips" under "Wholemeal Dough" p.133) to lighten the texture and flavour.

Organic & Dietary Tips

If you want wheat-free bread, bran should not be used, as it is a wheat product. Bran is a natural laxative.

CORNFLOUR BREAD

Use the basic wholemeal dough recipe or commercial variation, reduce flour content by 250 g and substitute with the same amount of cornflour. Replace 1 tbsp of honey with 2 tbsp of maple syrup and follow all other instructions.

Cook's Tips

For a traditional American wheat-free cornbread, use dough preparation method No 2, p.126, then:

- *Rub 10 g fresh yeast and 10 g butter (optional) into 450 g cornflour.*
- *Add 2 cups milk (or buttermilk if available in organic form), 2 eggs and 1 tsp salt and mix together.*
- *Let sit in a warm place for 35 minutes before baking. (If substituting baking soda for yeast, this is not necessary.)*
- *Knock back, knead and form into individual muffin shapes.*
- *Place on oiled or greased tray and bake in oven heated to 230°C for 30-35 minutes.*

NB: *This recipe dates back to the early 19th century.*

Organic & Dietary Tips

Cornflour bread can be used as a wheat-free bread (if using traditional recipe). Not suitable for non-dairy or salt-free diets.

MILLET BREAD

Use the wholemeal dough recipe, p.133, adding 225 g of millet flour, and follow all other instructions.

Cook's Tips

For a healthier bread, reduce flour by 225 g and substitute 110 g of wheatgerm. Millet bread can be cooked wheat-free if making flat bread. (See "Flat Bread" recipes, p.140-144.)

OAT FLOUR BREAD

Use the wholemeal dough recipe, p.133, adding 450 g of oat flour and 1 lightly-beaten egg, and follow all other instructions.

Cook's Tips

Oat flour dough can be added to almost any bread mixture to give more nutrition.

Organic & Dietary Tips

Can be used in wheat-free breads, but is not suitable on its own, in our opinion.

RICE BREAD

Using a wholemeal dough recipe, p.133, substitute rice flour for wheat flour, and follow other instructions, except for baking — the oven should be heated to 180°C and the loaf baked for 1 hour. Two raisings should be adequate, but dough will not double in size. This bread will be small in volume and close in texture. If wheat is not a problem for you, a bulkier texture can be obtained using a 50-50 mix of rice and wheat flour.

Cook's Tips

Rice flour, like millet or oats, can be added to any bread for more flavour.

Organic & Dietary Tips

Rice bread is an excellent-tasting, wheat-free product. Salt can be reduced but should not be eliminated.

RYE BREAD

Use the barley bread recipe, p.135, substituting rye for barley, and follow all other instructions.

Cook's Tips

- *For a lighter bread, or if you don't mind wheat, use Sourdough Starter (see Sourdough Bread recipe, p134) and a 50-50 mix of rye and wheat flour (total 1 kg).*
- *Mix half of the combined flours with 1 cup of starter and 1 cup of purified water and let sit it overnight.*
- *The next day, add the rest of the flour and all other ingredients listed in the barley bread recipe, except milk and yeast.*
- *For a better rise, at this point add a natural baking agent, eg, soda bicarbonate (optional).*
- *Let the mixture rise at least three times.*
- *After the second rise, knock back and knead, place in oiled or greased baking tins, or form into a round loaf on a flat surface.*
- *Cover with a wet towel and let rise for 1 hour before baking.*
- *Bake at 230ºC for 1 hour.*

NB: *A traditional rye bread usually contains caraway seeds, which are added to dough after mixing.*

Organic & Dietary Tips

This is an excellent wheat-free bread if using Method No 1, p.126. Rye and wheat flour can also be combined with other flours, eg, rice, wheat, barley, etc, for a more interesting taste.

SOYA BREAD

Add 100 g of soya flour to white bread dough recipe, p.132, reducing white flour to 575 g, and follow all other instructions. White flour is traditionally used, but you can also use the wholemeal dough recipe.

Cook's Tips

Like rice, rye and barley can be added to any wheat or non-wheat dough mix.

Organic & Dietary Tips

Soya flour is usually added to wheat products to enhance nutritional value. Soya bread is suitable for wheat-free diets.

TRITICALE BREAD

Prep time: 1 ¼ hours

Cooking time: 55-60 minutes

Number of servings: Depends on use (makes 1 loaf)

Shelf life: 5 days in refrigerator; otherwise 3

Utensils: Mixing bowl, loaf tin

Ingredients

Yeast (25 g fresh, 3 tsp dry)   1 ¾ cups water

¼ cup honey   2 tbsp oil

1 tsp salt   4 cups triticale flour

Method

Follow any of the dough preparation instructions, p.125-126. Knead once, place into the loaf tin for one raising, cover with wet towel and let sit in a warm place for 1 hour.

Bake at 230°C for 55-60 minutes.

Cook's Tips

Triticale is a delicate gluten and should be handled as little as possible. It raises best the first time, which is why it should only be kneaded once after mixing before raising. It is raised only in the baking tin, to keep handling to a minimum.

Organic & Dietary Tips

Triticale is not a wheat, but an accidental hybrid of wheat and rye, combining the high protein and lysine contents of both.

Flat Breads

Flat breads are an essential part of the meals of numerous countries, including India, Italy, Africa, the Middle East and South America. They are the oldest form of bread in the world and are frequently "unleavened", a biblical word meaning "free of yeast and other raising agents". These breads are quick and easy to make, and are suitable for people with allergies or on special diets.

MEXICAN TORTILLAS (Corn)

Prep time: 10 minutes
Cooking time: 2 minutes per tortilla
Number of servings: Makes 12-13 tortillas
Shelf life: Best served immediately; will keep for 3-5 days if refrigerated
Utensils: Mixing bowl, griddle or large iron frying pan

Ingredients

450 g cornflour

1 tsp salt

1 cup boiling water

2 tbsp lime or lemon juice

Method

Mix salt and cornflour together, pour boiling water and lime/lemon over cornflour and stir rapidly until well mixed, then work dough with hands. When you have an elastic but not sticky dough (add more cornflour if necessary), form into balls (golf ball size) with your hands and roll out onto a flour-coated surface in circular patterns about the size of a side plate.

Slightly oil griddle or pan and heat to medium-high. Cook tortillas on each side until brown "freckles" appear. Place in towel to keep warm and serve immediately.

Cook's Tips

Corn tortillas are often made with white flour in South America. If this flavour appeals to you, use a 50-50 mix of corn and white flour and follow all other instructions. Lard is often also used, but you can use butter instead. Add 25 g to the above recipe and another 25 g of cornflour.

Organic & Dietary Tips

Suitable for non-dairy and wheat-free diets.

SPECIAL NOTE: Authentic Tortillas from scratch

If you have the time and want to make tortillas the traditional way, this is how to do it!

- Begin with 1 kilo of dried corn kernels, 60 g of lime powder (available from hardware or garden stores), and 3 litres of purified water.
- Wash the corn, place in large pot, add water and lime and bring to boil until kernel skins loosen.
- Remove the mixture and cool, run corn between palms of your hands to loosen skins, rinse kernels thoroughly in cold water to remove lime.
- Drain and place the corn in a grinder, food processor/masticator or mortar and pestle and grind into soft dough.
- Form dough into balls and follow cooking instructions, p.140.

FLOUR TORTILLAS

Prep time: 50 minutes

Cooking time: 2 minutes per tortilla (see below)

Number of servings: Makes 12-13 tortillas

Shelf life: Best served immediately; will keep for 3-5 days if refrigerated

Utensils: Mixing bowl, griddle or large iron frying pan

Ingredients

475gs wheat or white flour
*   (preferably soft)*
1 tsp salt
1 tbsp baking soda

1 cup boiling purified water
25 g butter

Method

Mix salt, baking soda and flour together, rub in butter, pour in boiling water and stir rapidly until well-mixed, then work dough with hands. When you have an elastic but not sticky dough (add more flour if necessary), cover with wet towel and let sit for 40 minutes. Form dough into balls (golf ball size) with your hands and roll out onto a flour-coated surface in circular patterns about the size of a side plate.

Slightly oil griddle or pan and heat to medium-high. Cook tortillas on each side till brown "freckles" appear. Place in towel to keep warm and serve immediately.

Cook's Tips

Corn and flour tortillas can both be used for Mexican meals such as tacos, enchiladas or quesadillas and flour tortillas for burritos and chimichangas.

Organic & Dietary Tips

Not suitable for non-dairy or wheat-free diets.

INJERA BREAD *(Ethiopian)*

Prep time: 12 minutes plus 24 hours fermentation
Cooking time: 15-35 minutes (see below)
Number of servings: 12-15 portions
Shelf life: 3-5 days refrigerated
Utensils: Mixing bowl, large iron frying pan

Ingredients

675 g fine millet flour
1/4 tsp baking soda
2 tsp honey

1 tbsp dry yeast
5 cups purified water

Method

Place yeast in 1/4 cup of lukewarm water and stir in honey. When yeast is frothy and rising (approximately 5 minutes), combine with rest of water and stir in millet flour until mixed and lump free. Leave in warm place to ferment for 24 hours.

After fermenting, stir again and add baking soda, eliminating any lumps that have formed overnight. You should have a smooth batter similar to pancakes.

Oil pan and heat to medium-hot, quickly add 1/3 of a cup of batter, pouring from outer edge of pan in spiral motion towards centre. The bread should cook quickly, without browning. Cover pan and cook injera for approximately one minute. The bread should rise slightly and be removed with a spatula. The top should be slightly moist and the bottom dry, but not crisp or brown. Continue until all batter is used.

Place injera on a platter separately to cool before stacking for serving.

Cook's Tips

Injera bread is especially good with soups or stews — tear off a piece and use as a scoop for the filling. It can also be used as an alternative in Mexican or Indian dishes, or for a sandwich similar to pita bread.

Organic & Dietary Tips

Suitable for non-dairy and wheat-free diets.

CHAPATIS

Prep time: 40 minutes

Cooking time: 15 minutes (see below)

Number of servings:4-6

Shelf life: Use immediately

Utensils: Pot for boiling water, chopping board, mixing bowl, rolling pin, grill or frying pan

Ingredients

1 cup boiling purified water

3 cups wholemeal zintrofen flour or fine pastry flour

75 g unsalted butter

1/4 tsp salt

Method

Bring water to boil, mash butter into flour and salt, and add the water. This does most of the kneading for you. Knead dough until soft, then allow to set for about 20 minutes.

Important: Knead again until soft.

Heat grill or frying pan to medium. Roll dough into ping-pong size balls, then roll out very thin on flour-covered board.

Grill or fry for a maximum of one minute each side on a high heat, turning quickly to prevent burning. Serve immediately in a bread basket, wrapped in towel to keep hot.

Cook's Tips

Chapatis should be a light-brown speckled colour. Serve simply buttered, or with any Indian curry meal. Chapatis are great as an alternative to Mexican tortillas, in such dishes as enchiladas, quesadillas and burritos, and with soups.

Organic & Dietary Tips

For vegans, substitute 35ml of oil for butter. Reduce salt for low-sodium diet.

International Dishes

DIHE

Based on original Lake Chad recipe

Prep time: 15 minutes

Cooking time: 30 minutes

Number of servings: 4

Shelf life: Will refrigerate for 4 days approximately – best used immediately

Utensils: Saucepan, frying-pan, blender

Ingredients

1 cup millet, raw

*1/2 cup vegetable stock or
    purified water*

1 tbsp Spirulina

1/4 medium onion*

1 clove garlic*

*1/4 cup pimento
    (red chilli)**

1 medium capsicum*

Salt (approximately 1/4 tsp)

Method

Gently boil millet in covered saucepan for 30 minutes or until all water is dissolved. Meanwhile pre-blend stock/water with Spirulina, then sauté onions and garlic in frying pan for 60 seconds; add chopped pimento and capsicum, sauté another 30 seconds.

Add contents of the blender to the pan and stir to uniform consistency. Drain millet, cover with sauce and salt to taste.

Cook's Tips

This recipe suggests adding salt after cooking, but we feel it is better to add it while millet is boiling. Eat dihe as a meal by itself, or as a complement to other dishes.

Organic & Dietary Tips

Eliminate salt for low-sodium diets. Suitable for diabetics and vegans. A small hot pickled chilli may be substituted if organic pimentos unavailable — use your own judgment on toxicity.

* See Chart One: Seasonal Availability.

This recipe is courtesy of Life Stream Research, Auckland

LENTIL DHAL

Prep time: 10 minutes
Cooking time: 20-25 minutes
Number of servings: Up to 6 people, depending on use
Shelf life: Refrigerates for up to 1 week
Utensils: Frying-pan, pot, food processor

Ingredients

1 cup lentils	1 tsp sea salt
2 onions	1 tsp curry powder*
4-6 cloves garlic	2 cinnamon sticks or $^{1}/_{2}$ tsp powder
$^{1}/_{2}$ tsp cumin	1-2 cups fresh coriander leaves
2 fresh chillies	Grated coconut*

Method

Wash and cook lentils in salted purified water until soft. Meanwhile, heat enough oil for sautéing in a frying-pan. Add chopped onions and chillies and crushed garlic, sauté about two minutes, then add the remaining spices, except cinnamon and coriander. Sauté for another 30-60 seconds then place in food processor.

Add cinnamon to the lentils for the last five minutes of their cooking time. Drain lentils, retaining the liquid, then add the lentils to the food processor.

Chop coriander leaves (1-2 cups according to taste) and add to the food processor. Turn on the processor and mix ingredients, adding enough liquid to achieve a chunky paste.

Serve immediately while hot, or if serving later, save remaining liquid from cooking, as you will need to add a little moisture when re-heating. Sprinkle the top with coconut when serving.

Cook's Tips

Lentils can be soaked and sprouted instead of cooked. Retain soaking water for use when processing. Prepare other ingredients as above, adding salt and cinnamon during processing, and follow other instructions. Add more or use hotter chillies if a spicier dish is desired. Traditionally, the coconut is added to the dhal during cooking, but for this recipe the flavours have been kept separate to allow for individual tastes.

Lentil dhal is traditionally served with rice, stir-fried vegetables and pita bread. Can also be used as a dip, with chips or vegetables, or as a side dish with other Indian meals.

Organic & Dietary Tips

Suitable for diabetics and vegans. Reduce or eliminate salt for sodium-free diets.
* May not be available in organic form.

FALAFEL

Prep time: 15 minutes, plus overnight soaking
Cooking time: Nil
Number of servings: 6
Shelf life: Use immediately. Can be frozen — thaw before cooking

Ingredients

2¹/₂ cups chickpeas

2 medium onions or
  same amount of leeks

1¹/₂ cups fresh coriander

3 tbsp ground cumin

Organic oil for frying

¹/₄ tsp sea salt

Method

Soak chickpeas in purified water overnight, unless sprouting. Drain. Peel and quarter onions, or chop white parts only of leeks, place in food processor. Add remaining ingredients except chickpeas. Blend until finely chopped, then gradually add chickpeas until a slightly chunky paste is obtained.

Allow to stand for one hour, then using wet hands, form into patties or balls. Fry in hot oil until till golden brown on both sides.

Cook's Tips

If sprouting, see sprouting instructions in previous recipe and follow instead of soaking. If freezing for future use, make into desired shape before freezing.

Organic & Dietary Tips

Suitable for vegans and diabetics. Eliminate or reduce salt for low-sodium diets.
***NB:** Cumin is the only the ingredient not available in organic form in New Zealand.*

Falafel is excellent as a burger pattie, in pita bread sandwiches, in traditional Lebanese salads with yoghurt sauce (see recipe, p.164) and as a general meat alternative (eg, spaghetti and falafel balls).

HUMUS

Prep time: 15 minutes, plus overnight soaking
Cooking time: 60 minutes
Number of servings: About 8 people
Shelf life: Will refrigerate for up to 1 week

Ingredients

250 g chickpeas (garbanzo beans)

5 cloves garlic

*4-6 tbsp cold-press olive
    oil (according to taste)*

8 tbsp lemon juice

1/2 cup tahina paste

1 tsp sea salt

Method

Soak chickpeas in purified water overnight (unless sprouting, see below), drain and rinse, place in pot and cover with water, boil 45-60 minutes, adding water to avoid drying out. Chickpeas should be soft to the touch.

Drain and place in the food processor, add remaining ingredients, process at high speed at least 5 minutes or until a paste texture is achieved. Place in storage container and chill at least one hour before use.

Cook's Tips

Sprouting organic chickpeas before cooking can increase their already high nutritional value. To sprout the peas properly, soak between two damp cloths or paper towels, rinsing at least once a day until most have produced a small white root. When cooking sprouted peas, reduce boiling time to 30 minutes maximum.

Humus should have a strong lemon flavour, so add extra juice if desired. It can be used in Lebanese salads, as a dip, in sandwiches, on vegeburgers, with pita bread, or as a meal in itself.

For a genuine Lebanese meal, make a mound of humus on a plate, make hollow in centre with large spoon or ladle, fill hollow with cold-press olive oil and serve as a dip with pita or unleavened bread.

Organic & Dietary Tips

Suitable for vegans and diabetics, leave out or reduce salt for low-sodium diets. All ingredients available in organic form in New Zealand.

CHINESE RICE

Prep time: 5 minutes

Cooking time: 25 minutes

Number of servings: 4

Shelf life: Serve immediately, or use within 3 days if refrigerated

Utensils: Pot for cooking rice, large frying-pan or wok

Ingredients

1 cup long grain rice (brown)

1/4 tsp salt

1 clove garlic

1/2 onion

1 cup mixed carrot, celery and peas

3 tbsp shoyu sauce

1 tbsp honey

1 cup mung beans

Method

Place rice in 2 cups of purified water with salt and crushed garlic, bring to boil and cook 15-20 minutes.

Slice onion finely lengthways, chop carrot and celery. Place enough oil to sauté in frying-pan or wok, add all vegetables except mung beans and sauté for approximately two minutes until soft.

Add drained rice, shoyu and honey and stir-fry for approximately five minutes. Remove from the heat and add mung beans. Serve immediately.

Cook's Tips

This dish can be served with meat or egg. Cook the egg separately like an omelette, cut into long strips and add to the rice at the same time as the mung beans. This is to ensure the egg retains its own flavour.

If using any meat, always be sure it is pre-cooked and add during sautéing. Remember that shoyu has a strong, salty flavour and you may want to take this into account when adding salt to the rice, or add more for stronger flavour.

Chinese rice should be sweet, so vary the amount of honey according to taste. This dish can be served alone or with Chinese or any seafood dishes.

Organic & Dietary Tips

This recipe uses shoyu sauce because it is available in organic form, unlike soy sauce. Tamari can be substituted for shoyu. Not suitable for salt-free diets. Suitable for vegan and vegetarian diets.

TRADITIONAL SPANISH RICE

Prep time: 10 minutes
Cooking time: 30 minutes
Number of servings: 4
Shelf life: Serve immediately, use within 3 days if refrigerated
Utensils: Large frying-pan with lid

Ingredients

4 large ripe tomatoes

1 large onion

1 large chilli (any variety)

1 large green capsicum

4 cloves garlic

1 cup long grain rice (brown)

2 cups purified water

1 tsp salt

1 tsp honey

1/4 cup fresh coriander

Assorted vegetables

(See"Cook's Tips" below)

Method

Heat a suitable amount of oil in frying pan, add tomatoes whole with skins and sauté until skins loosen. Remove skins, then add chopped onion, chilli and capsicum and crushed garlic. Sauté a further 30-60 seconds, then add rice, cook until rice slightly darker in colour, stirring constantly (approximately 7-10 minutes).

Add 2 cups purified water and other ingredients except coriander, cover and bring to boil, then simmer until rice is cooked. Add chopped fresh coriander just before serving.

Cook's Tips

Depending on your own taste, use a mild or hot chilli (jalapeno is the best for authentic flavour). Other vegetables can be added to the rice, eg, zucchini, carrots and green peas. Add these when the rice is boiling. Zucchini can alternatively be sliced thinly and stirred in after rice is cooked.

If serving immediately hot, you can add more body by grating your favourite cheese and sprinkling it on top. Can be served alone, with Mexican dishes or as a side dish to any meal.

Organic & Dietary Tips

Suitable for vegans. Honey and salt can be eliminated — substitute 1/2 tsp basil and oregano for salt during sautéing.

RICE PATTIES

Prep time: 10 minutes

Cooking time: 20 minutes

Number of servings: Makes 10-15 patties

Shelf life: Can be frozen 5 days in refrigerator

Utensils: Mixing bowl, pot for boiling rice, frying-pan

Ingredients

2 cups brown short grain rice

1¾ cups purified water

¼ tsp sea salt

1-2 cloves garlic

¼ cup shredded carrot

½ medium onion or leek

⅛ cup chopped parsley

½ cup wholemeal flour

Method

Place rice, crushed garlic, water and salt into a pot, bring to the boil and simmer for 25 minutes. Meanwhile, shred carrot and finely chop the onion and parsley.

Drain cooked rice, mix with flour in bowl and add other ingredients. Shape patties with hands, then coat lightly with flour. Refrigerate or freeze until ready for use.

To cook patties, place in frying pan with preferred oil and fry till golden brown on both sides. Serve immediately.

Cook's Tips

Rice patties can be made wheat-free by using rice flour, but the patties should be fried immediately because texture will be less firm. You may also want a moister mixture. When freezing or refrigerating for later use, place ordinary or waxed paper between patties for easy separation.

Rice patties are delicious as a substitute for meat in burgers, shaped into smaller balls for use in salads, or by themselves with sauce or gravy.

Organic & Dietary Tips

Salt can be eliminated for sodium-free diets. Salt is not important to the flavour of this recipe. Suitable for vegans. All ingredients available organically in New Zealand.

ORGANIC TEX-MEX BURGERS

Prep time: 10 minutes

Cooking time: Approximately 7 minutes

Number of servings: 5

Shelf life: For eating immediately

Ingredients

500 g beef mince

1 tbsp cumin*

1/2 cup wheat flour

3 tbsp Worcestershire sauce*
or purified water

Method

Mix all ingredients thoroughly by hand; add water if necessary. Form into hamburger-size patties.

Fry or barbecue.

Cook's Tips

There is less shrinkage when cooking organic meat due to the lower fat content, so allow for this when forming patties.

Cumin may be increased according to taste, and the mixture can be spiced up with a teaspoon or more of chilli powder* or two medium-sized fresh chillies, minced.

Serve with Mexican chilli sauce for a traditional flavour. You can make your own by adding a teaspoon or more of dried chilli flakes to tomato sauce.

Tex-Mex patties are good for use in burgers or as a filler in tacos, enchiladas and other Mexican dishes.

Organic & Dietary Tips

* Not available in processed organic form.

FREE-RANGE SOUTHERN BARBECUED CHICKEN

Prep time: 15 minutes plus marinating time
Cooking time: 45 minutes baking, 30-40 minutes barbecue
Number of servings: 6
Shelf life: 4 days in refrigerator

Ingredients

2 No 8 chickens

1 small onion or leek*

4-5 cloves garlic

1 tbsp fresh oreganum

1 tsp mild chilli powder**
    (maximum) or 2 fresh
    chillies*, minced

1 tbsp paprika**

250gs tomato paste

2 tbsp apple cider vinegar

2 tbsp honey

1 tsp sea salt

1/4 cup shoyu or
    Worcestershire** sauce

Method

Halve the chicken or cut into appropriate sized pieces. Place on baking tray, preferably one that has a cover, or if for barbecue, place pieces in a bowl.

To make sauce, sauté chopped onions, crushed garlic, oregano, chilli and paprika together in oil until onion is soft, then add tomato paste and cook until bubbling (approximately five minutes). Combine with all other ingredients in a blender and mix until liquid. The liquid should be thick but not too pasty; add purified water to make suitable for marinating meat.

Pour sauce over the chicken and place in the refrigerator for at least 90 minutes. If baking, pre-heat oven to 200°C, place covered chicken in the oven for 30 minutes, remove cover and cook for remainder of baking time, taking care not to burn top of chicken.

For a barbecue, place chicken pieces on cooler part of the barbecue and cook covered for at least 25 minutes and uncovered for the remainder of the time. Turn occasionally to avoid burning.

Cook's Tips

Be sure that chicken has cooked properly; the meat should have shrunk on the bone and should not exude any blood. Pierce the meat if in doubt.

NB: *Free-range chicken usually has less fat under its skin, which is why the meat should be covered initially during cooking to avoid drying out. Cayenne pepper can be used instead of chilli powder, but half the amount, and maple syrup can be substituted for honey.*

This dish will taste better if allowed to marinate overnight. Baste with marinade during cooking.

Organic & Dietary Tips

If baking, skin can be removed for low-fat diets. Free-range chickens are readily available, but not necessarily in organically reared form.

* See Charts One and Two: Seasonal Availability, p.36-39.

** These products may not be available processed in organic form.

CHICKEN MOLE

Prep time: 20 minutes
Cooking time: Approximately 45 minutes
Number of servings: 4
Shelf life: Refrigerates for 3-4 days
Utensils: 1 large stainless steel or iron frying-pan, food processor or blender

Ingredients

*1 No 8 organically-reared
    or free-range chicken*
*1 tbsp sesame seeds or 2 tbsp
    organic nuts, eg, almonds,
    cashews*
10 medium fresh tomatoes
4-5 large jalapeno chillies
2 medium onions
6 cloves garlic
*5 tbsp unsweetened organic
    chocolate**

$^1/_2$ tsp cinnamon
$^1/_2$ tsp cumin
1 large tbsp honey
$^1/_2$ tsp sea salt
1 $^1/_2$ cups coconut milk*
1 cup fresh coriander leaves
*$^1/_2$ tbsp organic fine flour
    (optional)*
1 lemon

Method

Cut whole chicken into pieces and place in oiled baking pan. If using sesame seeds, toast in frying pan first at a moderate heat, constantly stirring until a slightly brown texture appears. If using nuts, toast in the oven then grind them to a chunky texture.

Heat oil in a frying-pan, add tomatoes and finely chopped chillies, cook over a moderate heat and remove tomato skins as they wrinkle. Add chopped onion and garlic, and sauté all ingredients for about 60 seconds. Increase heat, add chocolate, cinnamon, cumin, honey, salt and coconut milk. Bring to a boil on a medium-high heat, stir to avoid burning. When mixture is boiling, reduce heat and add flour. Mix to a creamy texture and simmer at a low heat for approximately five minutes.

Remove from the heat, add seeds or nuts and chopped coriander leaves. Mix, then place all ingredients in food processor or blender, processing for about 60 seconds.

Add more liquid at this stage if desired. The sauce should be pasty. Pour sauce over the chicken pieces.

A tip: *Don't discard the leftover sauce from the processor. Mix it with a little water and reserve to use when the chicken is cooking, to avoid drying out.*

Cover chicken, place in the refrigerator and leave for four hours, or overnight. When cooking the chicken, heat oven to 180°C, cover baking dish and bake for 45 minutes. Uncover for the last five minutes of baking if a crisper finish is preferred.

When serving, squeeze lemon over the top, or use as a garnish.

Cook's Tips

Use a baking tray with a cover rather than aluminium foil. Leftover chicken can be refrigerated and re-heated. Add liquid to replace moisture lost during refrigeration before re-heating.

Remember chicken is a major source of food poisoning. It should not be left at room temperature for more than two hours and should always be thoroughly re-heated. Traditionally, in Mexico, the chocolate comes in raw, hard form, but you can also purchase it in powdered form.

Serve Chicken Mole with rice, beans or a big green summer salad. The sauce can also be used with vegetarian dishes (eg, tofu), or on fish or enchiladas.

Organic & Dietary Tips

Salt can be eliminated for low-sodium diets and replaced with an equivalent amount of oreganum.

* At the time of writing, organic chocolate is available in New Zealand as unsweetened powder and in sweetened hard form. Coconut milk is not available in organic form at present — use only milk from fresh coconuts, not from a can.

CEVICHE

(South American Marinated Fish)

Prep time: 15 minutes

Marinating time: 6 hours minimum

Number of servings: 4

Shelf life: Refrigerates for 2 days

Utensils: Stainless steel or glass mixing bowl

Ingredients

5-6 fillets snapper	*2 large carrots*
4 large lemons or limes	*2 tomatoes*
1 tbsp apple cider vinegar	*1-2 fresh chillies*
(optional)	*1 green capsicum*
1 tsp salt	*¼ cup fresh coriander*

Method

Chop or grate fish fillets into small chunks and place in a bowl. Add juice of lemons or limes. (If using vinegar, use one less lemon or lime and add at this point.) Add salt, grated carrots and very finely chopped tomatoes, chilli and capsicum. Mix thoroughly, cover and place in the refrigerator.

Stir occasionally while marinating so that the juice does not settle to the bottom. Add fresh coriander, finely chopped, just before serving.

Cook's Tips

When using coriander with any meal, use only leaves, not stems, as these have a bitter taste. The amount of chillies used depends on personal taste.

Serve with corn chips or for the traditional touch, on a "tostada" (flat deep-fried corn tortilla) with a little Mexican hot sauce on top. An American version is to spread mayonnaise on the tostada. Ceviche can also be served on top of salad.

FISH IN ORGANIC WINE

Prep time: 10 minutes
Cooking time: 11 minutes
Number of servings: 4
Shelf life: Eat immediately
Utensils: Large frying-pan, with lid

Ingredients

1/2 small onion

4 cloves garlic

1 tbsp butter

4 fillets snapper

1 1/2 cups organic chardonnay

Thyme

Salt & pepper

8 fresh mint leaves

Method

Finely chop onion, grind garlic. Place a little cooking oil in the pan with butter, bring to moderate heat and place fish fillets in pan, along with onion and garlic.

Cover and cook for five minutes, turn, add wine, a pinch of thyme and 2 mint leaves on each fillet, plus salt and pepper to taste, and cook another 6-7 minutes. Serve immediately.

Cook's Tips

Serve with salad or fluffy brown organic rice.

Organic & Dietary Tips

Assuming the fish was free-ranged, all other products should be obtainable in organic form.

ORGANIC FISH BATTER

For the fish 'n' chips fanatics, here's a good beer batter recipe using organic ingredients:

Mix one cup of organic pastry flour and 1/2 cup of organic bran with 1/4 tsp each of salt and pepper, one free-range egg (yolk only) and 1/2 cup of beer. Use as you would any batter, deep-frying in oil.

TOFU KEBABS

Prep time: 10 minutes

Cooking time: 4-6 minutes

Number of servings: 10 kebabs

Shelf life: Best fresh! Refrigerates for up to 3 days

Utensils: Stainless steel or bamboo skewers

Ingredients

1 kg tofu

1/4 cup shoyu or
        Worcestershire* sauce

1 medium onion

1 zucchini

4-5 medium tomatoes

2 capsicums

Method

Cut tofu into equal-sized cubes (three per kebab), pour shoyu or Worcestershire sauce into a bowl, place tofu in bowl and marinate while preparing other ingredients.

Halve onion, then divide each half into thirds and separate the layers. Slice zucchini, quarter tomatoes, seed capsicum and cut into chunks. Thread alternately onto skewers. (Make them colourful!) Place on grill and cook for 4-6 minutes.

Cook's Tips

Tofu should be warmed up rather than cooked in this recipe, to enhance the flavour. Avoid over-cooking.

Serve tofu kebabs with stir-fried vegetables and/or salad.

* Not available organically.

TOFU MAYONNAISE

Prep time: 10 minutes
Cooking time: Nil
Number of servings: Makes 350 ml
Shelf life: Refrigerates for up to 4 weeks
Utensils: Food processor or blender, 350 ml glass storage container

Ingredients

200 gm drained or pressed tofu

2 tbsp vinegar

1/2 tsp salt or 2 tbsp shoyu or
    1 tbsp red miso

1/2-1 tsp mustard (optional)*

2 tbsp lemon juice

2-4 tbsp cold-press safflower
    or flax seed oil

1 tsp honey (optional)

Method

Combine all ingredients in a blender or processor and pureé for 30-60 seconds until texture is smooth and even.

Cook's Tips

Add crushed garlic for a more European flavour. Oil can be left out but will definitely affect the texture. Shoyu and miso are both salt substitutes, but also add special flavours.

Use tofu mayonnaise as a salad dressing or in sandwiches, and as a basis for other sauces.

Organic & Dietary Tips

Suitable for diabetics and vegans if honey eliminated.

* May not be available in organic form.

TOMATO SAUCE

Prep time: 15-20 minutes
Cooking time: 45 minutes
Number of servings: Depends on use (makes 2 litres)
Shelf life: Refrigerates for approximately 2 months
Utensils: Large stainless steel pot for boiling, food processor or masticating juicer, cotton cloth or cheesecloth

Ingredients

12 ripe tomatoes	*1 tbsp celery seed*
4 large onions	*1 tbsp mustard seed*
4 cloves garlic	*1 cinnamon stick**
1 tbsp salt	*8 peppercorns**
2 red peppers (optional)	*2 cups apple cider vinegar*
1 bay leaf	*1-1 1/2 cups honey*
1 small chilli	

Method

Place tomatoes in boiling water for a few seconds to loosen skin, remove skin and place in a stainless steel pot. Add chopped onions, garlic, salt and red peppers (optional), bring to the boil and simmer for 15 minutes.

Place in a food processor and mix to a juice before returning to the pot. In a cloth, place bayleaf, chilli, celery and mustard seeds, cinnamon stick and peppercorns, and tie with a cotton thread. Add this to the pot with the juiced ingredients, stir in the vinegar and honey and bring to boil again.

Simmer at a moderate heat for 25 minutes, stirring frequently to prevent scorching. If a sweeter sauce is preferred, add more honey at this stage. Remove spice bag after 25 minutes, and allow mixture to cool.

Cook's Tips

If sauce is not thick enough, add 1-2 tbsp cornstarch mixed in 2-4 tbsp water in last 2-3 minutes of cooking time. Tomato sauce can also be stored in preserving jars — place in sterilised jars while still hot.

Organic & Dietary Tips

*Salt can be reduced or removed by adding a little oregano and sweet basil, dry or fresh. *May not be available in organic form.*

QUICK TOMATO SAUCE

For a simpler recipe:

- Substitute a 250 g jar of organic tomato paste for raw tomatoes.
- Sauté 1/4 cup chopped onion, 2 cloves of pressed garlic, and 1/2 tsp dry or fresh basil and oregano in olive oil until soft.
- Add tomato paste, 1/2 tsp salt, 1/4 tsp black pepper*, 2 tbsp apple cider vinegar and 1 tbsp honey (or to taste).
- Cook gently for 20-25 minutes, stirring frequently. Cool and refrigerate.

May not be available in organic form.

GOOD EARTH MAYONNAISE

Prep time: 10 minutes
Cooking time: Nil
Number of servings: Makes 350 ml
Shelf life: Refrigerates for up to 4 weeks
Utensils: Food processor, 350-ml glass storage container

Ingredients

2 cups cold press rape seed oil

2 organic free-range eggs

4 tbsp apple cider vinegar

1-2 tsps honey

1 tsp mustard

1 tsp salt

Method

Put 1/3 cup of oil in the food processor, add two egg whites and one yolk only (the rest is not needed). Add vinegar, honey, mustard and salt and blend at high speed, dribbling remainder of oil into mixture over at least two minutes. With this method, the longer you take, the creamier the texture of the mayonnaise.

Cook's Tips

For a European-style Garlic Mayonnaise, add 4 cloves of crushed garlic before blending, then continue as before.

Good Earth mayonnaise can be used as a salad dressing, or in sandwiches — and it is great with tuna or devilled eggs.

Organic & Dietary Tips

Not suitable for vegans or diabetics.

QUICK AND EASY THOUSAND ISLAND & SEAFOOD DRESSING

Prep time: 10 minutes
Cooking time: Nil
Number of servings: According to quantities used
Shelf life: Refrigerates for up to 4 weeks
Utensils: Mixing bowl, suitable glass storage container

Ingredients

3 parts tomato sauce*

Oreganum

Sweet & Sour Gherkins**

5 parts Good Earth Mayonnaise, p.161

Pepper (For Seafood Dressing)

Method

Mix tomato sauce and mayonnaise, with seasoning to taste. Quantities can be varied according to amount of dressing needed.

If making Seafood Dressing, add chopped gherkins, with some of their juice to taste.

Cook's Tips

For a connoisseur's Thousand Island Dressing, stew needed quantity of tomatoes, remove skin, place in a blender, add garlic, salt and honey to taste and mix well. Use in place of tomato sauce and proceed with instructions above.

Thousand Island Dressing makes an excellent addition to salads, hamburgers and seafood.

Organic & Dietary Tips

Not suitable for vegans or diabetics.

* Refer to tomato sauce recipe or use commercial brand. (See "Chart Eight: Processed Foods & Beverages", p.44-46.)

** If buying commercially, refer to chart on "Processed Foods & Beverages", p.44-46. If making fresh, refer to "Chart One: Seasonal Availability" p.36-37 and section on "Bottling" p.48-55.

ITALIAN DRESSING (Oil-free)

Prep time: 10 minutes

Cooking time: 7 minutes

Number of servings: Depends on use

Shelf life: Refrigerates for up to 1 month

Utensils: Garlic crusher, frying-pan, 600-ml glass storage container

Ingredients

1 small red chilli*

500 ml apple cider vinegar

4 cloves garlic

1 tsp fresh oreganum

1 tsp fresh sweet basil

Pinch of salt

1 tbsp honey

2 bayleaves

Method

Fry chilli (preferably in an old pan) with no oil for 7 minutes, until dark on one side. Place half of the vinegar in a storage container, add crushed garlic with juice to vinegar, then chop and add oreganum and basil with salt and honey. Add whole bayleaves.

Shake well, then add rest of the vinegar and shake again. Preferably store overnight before use.

Cook's Tips

Using dried herbs extends the shelf life of dressings. If a milder taste is desired, use only half a chilli.

This recipe can be used in sandwiches, as a salad dressing, and as a marinade for raw seafood, cucumbers, or vegetables.

Organic & Dietary Tips

Not suitable for diabetics, salt can be left out for low-sodium diets.
Suitable for vegans.

* See "Chart One: Seasonal Availability", p.36-37.

QUICK AND EASY FRENCH DRESSING

Prep time: 5 minutes
Cooking time: Nil
Number of servings: Depends on use
Shelf life: Refrigerates for up to 6 weeks
Utensils: 200-ml glass container

Ingredients

1/2 cup cold press safflower oil

3 tbsp organic white wine

5 tbsp apple cider vinegar

Sea salt & pepper* to taste

Method

Mix ingredients in container; shake before serving.

Cook's Tips

Use this recipe as a salad and general dressing.

Organic & Dietary Tips

Suitable for vegans and diabetics.

* Not available in organic form.

LEBANESE YOGHURT SAUCE

Prep time: 15 minutes
Cooking time: Nil
Number of servings: Depends on use
Shelf life: Best used immediately; will last up to 1 week in the refrigerator
Utensils: Mixing bowl, garlic crusher

Ingredients

500gm natural Bulgarian or acidophilus yoghurt**

3 cloves garlic

2 medium lemons*

Method

Place yoghurt in a bowl, add crushed garlic and juice of lemons and stir. Let sit for 20 minutes before serving.

Cook's Tips

Serve this sauce with Lebanese falafel or over humus, as a dressing on any salad or seafood dish, and in vegetarian sandwiches.

Organic & Dietary Tips

A good sauce for diabetics and people on low-sodium diets.

*** See Chart Eight: "Processed Foods & Beverages", p.44-46.*
** See Chart Two: "Seasonal Availability", p.36-37.*

HOT JALAPENO SAUCE

Prep time: 15 minutes
Cooking time: 15 minutes
Number of servings: Depends on use
Shelf life: Refrigerates for up to 3 weeks
Utensils: Blender, frying-pan, 1-litre storage container

Ingredients

6 jalapeno chillies*
900 ml preserved whole
    tomatoes in juice*
1/8 cup apple cider vinegar
1 heaped tbsp honey

5 cloves garlic
1 tsp sea salt
1 cup fresh coriander
1 medium onion*

Method

Fry chillies (preferably in an old pan) with no oil for 15 minutes until black on two sides. Place 1/8 cup of the tomatoes in juice in the blender, together with vinegar, honey, peeled garlic and salt. Blend well for 60 seconds.

Stop the blender, then add ingredients to the mixture in the following order: chillies, coriander, the rest of the tomatoes and onion, chopped in large pieces.

Turn blender on and off five times or until all is mixed well.

Cook's Tips

The blender should be turned on and off to ensure the sauce remains chunky while becoming well-mixed.

Hot Jalapeno sauce makes a great Mexican hot sauce for corn chips, and can be added to any Mexican or Latin meals and sauces.

Organic & Dietary Tips

Honey can be left out for diabetics and sodium content reduced by leaving out the salt and adding more garlic and 1/4 tsp oreganum* (can be sautéed together for added flavour).

Suitable for Vegans
** See Chart One: "Seasonal Availability", p.36-37.*

TACO SAUCE (Mild)

Prep time: 15 minutes
Cooking time: Nil
Number of servings: Depends on use
Shelf life: Refrigerates for up to 4 weeks
Utensils: Blender, 1-litre storage container

Ingredients

2 jalapeno chillies
$1/2$ tsp sea salt
1 tbsp honey
$1/8$ cup apple cider vinegar
4 cloves garlic

$2/3$ cup fresh coriander
1 level tbsp oreganum
*900 ml preserved whole tomatoes
    in juice**
1 medium-small onion*

Method

Place chillies, salt, honey, vinegar and peeled garlic in a blender. Blend well for 60 seconds. Stop blender, then add ingredients in the following order: coriander, oreganum, tomatoes in juice and onion, chopped in large pieces. Turn the blender on and off three-to-five times until well-mixed.

Cook's Tips

The blender should be turned on and off to ensure the sauce remains chunky while becoming well-mixed.

Taco sauce can be used as as mild Mexican sauce on tacos or tostadas, as a sauce on Spanish or Mexican-style rice, as a traditional Latin seafood sauce on dishes such as Camorones Rancheros (prawns) or as a mild hot sauce for chips and nachos.

Organic & Dietary Tips

Honey can be omitted for diabetics and the sodium content reduced by leaving out the salt and adding more garlic with $1/4$ tsp of oreganum (sautéd together for added flavour).
Suitable for vegans

* See Chart One: "Seasonal Availability", p.36-37.

ENCHILADA SAUCE

Prep time: 20 minutes

Cooking time: 25 minutes

Number of servings: Depends on use — up to 25 enchiladas

Shelf life: Refrigerates for up to three weeks

Utensils: Large stainless steel saucepan, blender, 1-litre storage container

Ingredients

1 medium onion*

5 cloves garlic

Safflower oil or canola (unrefined)
as needed to sauté

1/6 cup hot jalapeno salsa
(See recipe, p.165)

900 ml preserved whole
tomatoes in juice*

1/2 tsp sea salt

1 level tbsp honey

1/8 cup apple cider vinegar

1/4 cup of purified water

5 tbsp wholemeal flour

1 cup fresh chopped coriander

Method

Peel and chop onion and garlic, place with oil in a large pot, sauté until the onion is soft. Add hot sauce, sauté for 30 seconds more, than add whole tomatoes with juice, salt, honey and vinegar.

Bring to the boil and simmer briskly for 20 minutes, stirring occasionally. Blend water and flour together for 90 seconds or until well mixed and add to simmering pot. Lower heat and simmer for five minutes, stirring frequently to avoid burning.

Remove from the heat and stir in coriander, then place the sauce in a blender and blend for 60 seconds, or until puréed.

Cook's Tips

Ensure flour and water is well-blended, the add the mixture slowly to the sauce while stirring constantly, to avoid lumps.

Pour this sauce over your favourite enchiladas. It is also excellent on nachos, and as a sauce in South American seafood and poultry dishes.

Organic & Dietary Tips

Honey can be omitted for diabetics and the sodium content reduced by leaving out the salt and adding more garlic and 1/4 tsp oreganum. (These can be sautéd with the onion for added flavour.)

Suitable for vegans

* See Chart One: "Seasonal Availability".

CURRY POWDER

Organic curry powder is not available in New Zealand at time of writing, but we consider it only a small ingredient of any curry dish, being used mostly for flavouring, like salt, pepper, honey, etc. Therefore, if your other ingredients (meat, vegetables, rice, water, etc) are all organic, the toxicity contribution (from the curry powder) will be minimal. Some of the ingredients for it are already available in organic form, and others may be in the future. For this reason we have included this basic recipe for making curry powder.

Prep time: 5-10 minutes
Number of servings: May serve more than 6 depending on use
Shelf life: Store as a herb for up to 4 months
Utensils: Blender or food processor, or mortar and pestle

Ingredients

4 dried curry leaves

1 tsp dry chilli*

1 tsp turmeric

175 g cumin

1 tsp dried coriander

Method

Combine all ingredients in a blender, food processor or mortar, and mix or grind into a fine powder.

Cook's Tips

Like coffee beans, freshly-ground curry powder should be used immediately for the best flavour. The stated amounts of ingredients will give you a mild to moderately hot curry. For more heat, add more chilli. For a milder taste, add more cumin rather than cutting back on the chilli.

To obtain the ingredients in organic form, you will most likely have to buy them fresh. At time of writing, curry leaves, coriander and chillies are available in organic form. Refer to section on "Preserving Herbs", p.56, for information on processing these

ingredients. Cumin seeds and turmeric may be available in the future in organic form.

Organic & Dietary Tips

Suitable for most diets.
*Refer to chart on "Seasonal Availability", p.36-37.

CREAMY PUMPKIN SOUP

(Non-dairy)

Prep time: 15 minutes

Cooking time: 25 minutes

Number of servings: 6

Shelf life: Refrigerates for up to one week

Utensils: Food processor, large stainless steel cooking pot,
1-litre glass storage container

Ingredients

1 kg pumpkin

2 medium potatoes

4 cloves garlic

1 medium onion* or same
  quantity leeks

1 1/2 tsp dry** or
  chopped fresh sweet basil

1/2 tsp dry oreganum**

Purified water

1 tsp honey

Pinch of pepper**

2 bayleaves**

1/4 tsp salt

Organic safflower oil for frying

Method

Peel pumpkin, remove seeds and chop into small cubes. Dice potatoes. Place oil in cooking pot, add crushed garlic, chopped onion or leeks, and sauté until soft but not brown.

Add oreganum and dry sweet basil. (If using fresh basil, add later according to the following instructions.) Sauté for a further 15 seconds, add two cups of water, honey, salt, pepper and bayleaves (and basil if using fresh), stir, and bring to boil. Add pumpkin and potatoes, then add water till half covered. Bring back to the boil, then cover and cook at a medium heat for 25 minutes.

Remove from heat, remove bayleaves, then place the mixture in a food processor. Process at high speed for 60 seconds, then serve immediately or place in a storage container to cool and reheat later. Sprinkle with paprika and fresh parsley when serving.

Cook's Tips

Pumpkin is best peeled whole. To peel the pumpkin, use a short-bladed, rigid vegetable knife. Hold the pumpkin by the stem, insert knife sideways just below skin, and peel down toward base. Repeat all the way around and peel off the ends while still whole. Then chop in half, remove seeds and cut into cubes.

Suitable for vegans. Eliminate honey for diabetics, and remove or reduce salt for low-sodium diets.

* See Chart One: "Seasonal Availability", p.36-37.
** May not be available in organic form.

Sweet Recipes

HONEY ICE-CREAM

Prep time: 15 minutes, plus freezing
Cooking time: 10 minutes
Number of servings: 3-4 (makes 500 ml)
Utensils: Large stainless steel saucepan, freezing container

Ingredients

2 free-range eggs   *2 cups organic cream**
1 cup organic raw milk   *1/2 tsp natural vanilla*
1/2 cup liquid honey   *1/4 tsp salt*

Method

Mix egg yolks and milk together, place in a saucepan and heat gently, stirring continually until bubbles break the surface. Do not simmer or boil. Stir in honey, remove from heat, allow to cool, then place in a freezing container and freeze for 30-45 minutes, or until the edges start to set.

Whip egg whites, and then whip cream and vanilla together and fold the two mixtures together. Remove mixture from freezer and fold all together. Place in a low shelf of the freezer for several hours.

For flavour variations, use the basic recipe, leaving out the vanilla extract, and adding different ingredients, such as chocolate, spices, and fruits and nuts. For a healthier dessert, change the dairy products; eg, replace the cream with yoghurt.

Organic & dietary Tips

Not suitable for vegans or diabetics.

* Not always readily available.

APPLE CAKE

Prep time: 15 minutes

Cooking time: 40 minutes

Number of servings: Depends on use

Shelf life: Will refrigerate for 5 days

Utensils: Mixing bowl, egg beater, deep baking dish

Ingredients

175 g wholemeal flour

75 g butter

*1 tbsp baking powder (optional)^*

5 tbsp honey

2 medium eggs

1 heaped tsp cinnamon+

700 g apples*

Method

Sift flour, cut in butter, add baking powder (if using), honey, eggs, cinnamon and peeled and diced apples, then mix and knead into a stiff dough.

Place in baking dish and bake at 180°C for 40 minutes.

Cook's Tips

Serve with organic cream or ice-cream

Organic & Dietary Tips

* See Chart Two: Seasonal Availability, p.36-37.

^ Not available in organic form.

+ Use your discretion about toxicity of cinnamon if not available in organic form.

Not suitable for vegans.

SPIRULINA FUDGE BROWNIES

Prep time: 15 minutes

Cooking time: 25 minutes

Number of servings: Depends on use

Shelf life: 4 days

Utensils: Food processor (not essential) or mixing bowl, shallow baking tray (approximately 20 X 30 cm).

Ingredients

2/3 cup unsweetened chocolate or carob

250 g butter

1 cup honey

5 medium eggs

1 1/2 tbsp real vanilla essence

1 tbsp Spirulina

1 cup wholemeal flour

Method

If using a food processor, melt the chocolate and allow to cool. Meanwhile cream butter, honey and eggs in processor, add vanilla and Spirulina while creaming. If using carob, mix to a paste with purified water in a cup. Add chocolate or carob and flour to other ingredients and mix well.

Spread in buttered baking tray and bake at 180°C for 25 minutes.

Without a food processor: Soften butter — do not melt. Place in mixing bowl with honey and eggs and cream together. Then follow the remaining instructions above.

Cook's Tips

If using carob, mix with milk rather than water for a creamier taste. Other types of flour can be substituted (eg, rye) or flour can be mixed with bran — with proportions to your taste.

Organic & Dietary Tips

At time of writing, chocolate and carob cannot be guaranteed organic. Use your discretion, but we believe carob has less toxicity. Rice flour can be substituted to make the recipe wheat-free. Suitable for low-sodium diets. Not suitable for vegans.

(This recipe is courtesy of Life Stream Research, Auckland)

SPIRULINA SMOOTHIE

Prep time: 4 minutes
Cooking time: Nil
Number of servings: 1
Shelf life: Drink immediately
Utensils: Blender

Ingredients

1 litre chilled juice of choice
    (orange, apple,
      kiwifruit, etc)
1 tbsp Spirulina

1 banana*
$1/2$ lemon
3-4 ice cubes

Method

Put all ingredients in blender and mix well.

Organic & Dietary Tips

*See Chart Two: "Seasonal Availability", p.36-37.
Suitable for all diets. Organic bananas are rarely available and you will most likely have to compromise on this ingredient.

This recipe is courtesy of Life Stream Research, Auckland

Index

The Organic Directory

Maid buying meat from butcher's boy, 1907

Accommodation/Farmstay

Blackrocks Farm

Naturally therapeutic. If your heart's in the country let the peace of this waterfront hideaway weave its spell, with its soft tides, green pastures and gentle animals. To recuperate from stress or illness:
Phone (09) 407 8660 or write to Penelope S Barnaby, Blackrocks Farm, PO Box 345, Kerikeri, Bay of Islands.
Bookings essential

Kimi Ora Holiday and Health Resort

Relax! Get Healthy! Get Pampered! Exquisite vegetarian cuisine fresh from our organic BIO-GRO gardens. Detox and juice fasts, Naturopathy, fitness trails, gym, sauna, swimming pool, tennis courts.
For bookings contact: Dietmar, Phone (03) 527 8027, Fax (03) 527 8134 or write C/- Post Office Kaiteriteri, Nelson Bay.

Our Farm-Park

Farmstay the gentle way, organic farming at Puhoi (Auckland). Comfortable beds — share tasty (organic) meals, panoramic views, fresh air (smoke free), clean water, peacefulness. Milk cow (we make butter, yoghurt, ice-cream, cheeses), horses to ride.
Phone (09) 422 0626/Fax (09) 422 0677 E-Mail ofp@friends.co.nz

Organic Suppliers

Bioshop

For all your organic food supplies. All products certified organic under Demeter, Bio Gro or International trademarks (or made from certified ingredients). Also Weleda products and Jurlique Skin Care.
Shop 4, 124 Opawa Road, Christchurch 2 Phone (03) 337 0022

Ceres Organics

Biodynamic and Organic Foods distributed nationwide. (See our advertisement for full details.)
**Retail: 181 Ladies Mile, Ellerslie
Phone (09) 579 7126 Fax (09) 525 5509
Warehouse: 3/10 Olive Road, Penrose
PO Box 11-336, Auckland 5
Phone (09) 579 6175 Fax (09) 0800 282 624**

Commonsense Organics

For all your culinary requirements. From fresh organic fruit, vegetables and herbs, milk, cheese, oils, through environmentally friendly cleaning products, vitamins and mineral supplements, shampoos and toilet soaps, to organic seeds and plantfood for organic home gardeners and more.
(See our full page advertisement opposite).
cnr Wakefield & Chaffers Streets, Wellington.
Free delivery within the Wellington city area.
Phone (04) 384 3314 Fax (04) 385 3383

Harmony Naturals

Nothing added — nothing removed. BIO-GRO Certified fresh flax seed oil and capsules. Kenkal process flours: fine and medium ground, hard, soft, Durum and Spelt wheats, rye and naked barley.
Waihi Bush, 21 RD, Geraldine
Phone (03) 6922 842 Fax (03) 6922 849

Harvest Wholefoods

New Zealand's most comprehensive range of organics, macrobiotics, natural foods and remedies. Foods for allergy sufferers, vegetarian take-aways, organic fruit and vegetables. PLUS an in-store Naturopath.
405 Richmond Road, Grey Lynn, Auckland Phone (09) 376 3107
Fax (09) 360 1616

Hislop's Wholefoods

Producers and stockists of Organic foods with main product lines carrying BIO-GRO certification. Producers of Stoneground flour, wholemeal bread. LICENSED CAFE — wines, beers and ales and vegetarian, meat and seafood. Get the REAL TASTE with ORGANICS.
Hislop's Wholefoods Ltd, Main South Road, R.D. 2, KAIKOURA, Ph & Fax (03) 319 5557 — Paul Hislop
CAFE, 33 Beach Road, Kaikoura; Ph (03) 319 6971

❦
For all your
ORGANIC
culinary requirements

❦ *in season fresh organic fruit, vegetables and herbs,* ❦ *organic milk, cheese, butter, eggs, yoghurt, soya milk and tofu,* ❦ *freshly baked from organic flour - breads, pasta, chapati, pizza bases carrot cakes and rich dark fruit cakes,* ❦ *organic flours and grains, dried pulses and pasta, dried fruit, breakfast cereals, muesli, dried herbs and spices,* ❦ *organic oils, vinegars, sugars, salt, tea, herb tea, coffee and coffee substitutes,* ❦ *organic wines, grape juice, fruit juices and other beverages,* ❦ *organic sausages, mince, chops, steaks, chickens, bacon and hams,* ❦ *organic honey, jams, chutney, pasta sauces, tomato paste, miso and vegetable concentrate,* ❦ *tinned organic tomato, asparagus, corn, beans, chickpeas and refried beans ,* ❦ *and more -*

plus

❦ *environmentally friendly cleaning products and washing powders,* ❦ *vitamins and mineral supplements,* ❦ *shampoos and toilet soaps,* ❦ *pure cotton tampons and sanitary pads,* ❦ *organic seeds and plantfood for organic home gardeners,* ❦ *and more -*

**Free delivery within the Wellington city area.
EFTPOS available.**

Ph (04) 384 3314 ❦ Fax (04) 385 3383

cnr Wakefield & Chaffers St., Wellington

CERTIFIED ORGANIC

For your supplies
of Certified Organic
Flours, Rolled Oats,
Grains & Wholefoods
Contact: NZ Biograins Ltd
P O Box 526, Ashburton
Ph/fax: (03) 308 7349

The Bio-gro symbol on food is your independent assurance that it is the product of organic agriculture.

NEW ZEALAND BIO GRAINS LTD

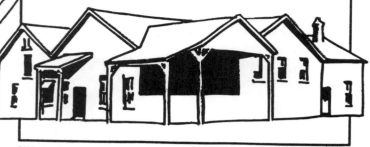

WEST STREET ASHBURTON

GROWN ON FARMS CERTIFIED BY THE N.Z. BIOLOGICAL PRODUCERS COUNCIL

Huckleberry Farms

Natural Food Supermarket. A complete range of fresh and prepared foods, as well as all your health and beauty care products makes this your one-stop organic shop. Parking right outside — off the road. (See our advertisement on the inside back cover.)
**Huckleberry Farms,
240 Greenlane Road West, Auckland
Phone (09) 630 8857 Fax (09) 630 8859**

NZ Bio Grains Ltd

For your supplies of BIO-GRO certified **ORGANIC FLOURS, ROLLED OATS, GRAINS AND WHOLEFOODS.**
(See full page advertisement opposite.)
**New Zealand Bio Grains Ltd,
West Street, Ashburton
P O Box 526, ASHBURTON
Phone/Fax (03) 308 7349**

Phoenix Natural Foods Ltd • Phone (09) 836 2272
P.O. Box 20-217, Glen Eden, Auckland, N.Z.

Phoenix Natural Foods Ltd

Hand made organic **PRESERVES** — 100% natural. Honey sweetened. Made in New Zealand from BIO-GRO Certified fruit. Also **NATURAL DRINKS**: Mineral Water both plain and naturally flavoured with Feijoa or Melon. Also Cola, Lemonade and Ginger Beer.
NO ARTIFICIAL FLAVOURS OR PRESERVATIVES ADDED.
Call or write for the name of your nearest stockist:
**Phoenix Natural Foods Ltd,
P O Box 20 217, Glen Eden, Auckland.
Ph (09) 836 2272 Fax (09) 836 5232**

Growers and Suppliers

Drinks
Phoenix Natural Foods Ltd

Hand made organic **PRESERVES** — 100% natural. Honey sweetened. Made in New Zealand from BIO-GRO Certified fruit. Also **PHOENIX NATURAL DRINKS**: Mineral Water both plain and naturally flavoured with Feijoa or Melon. Also Cola, Lemonade and Ginger Beer.
NO ARTIFICIAL FLAVOURS OR PRESERVATIVES ADDED. NATURALLY SWEETENED WITHOUT SUGAR
Call or write for the name of your nearest stockist:
**Phoenix Natural Foods Ltd,
P O Box 20 217, Glen Eden, Auckland.
Ph (09) 836 2272 Fax (09) 836 5232**

Eggs
Pukatea Orchard

BIO-GRO certified fruit, vegetables and eggs available all year round. Stock/price list available on request.
**Brian & Diane Renwick
98 Abel Tasman Drive, Takaka
Phone/Fax (03) 525 8237**

Fruit and vegetables
Kerikeri Organic Fruit

Freshly picked and sent to your door. We supply throughout the year: mandarins, Navel oranges, Sweet Tangelos and Valencia Oranges.
10kg — N.Island $20; S.Island $25 (inc. Freight)
**R de Boer, Mill Lane, Kerikeri
Phone (09) 407 9802**

Kerikeri Organic Fruit & Vegetables

Market garden and orchard. Organically grown fruit and vegetables available delivered fresh to your door. Wholesale or retail from brassicas and root crops to pumpkins and glasshouse crops.
Bulls Road, S H 10, Kerikeri, Bay of Islands. Call Marty or Tina Robinson or Grant Steven Phone/Fax (09) 407 8650

Kerimere Orchard

Absolutely yummy Navel and Valencia oranges, sweet mandarins and kiwifruit delivered to your door. All Certified organic and Bio-Dynamic, and available all year round for health and enjoyment.
**David and Priscilla Skinner
Kerimere Orchard, Riddell Road,
Kerikeri Phone/Fax (09) 407 9424**

Pukatea Orchard

BIO-GRO Certified fruit, vegetables and eggs available all year round. Stock/price list available on request.
**Brian & Diane Renwick
98 Abel Tasman Drive, Takaka
Phone/Fax (03) 525 8237**

Grains
NZ Bio Grains Ltd

For your supplies of BIO-GRO certified **ORGANIC FLOURS, ROLLED OATS, GRAINS AND WHOLEFOODS.
New Zealand Bio Grains Ltd,
West Street, Ashburton
P O Box 526, ASHBURTON
Phone/Fax (03) 308 7349**

Honey
Sensational Kiwi Honeys

BIO-GRO certified organic Bee Pollen. Great as a health and energy supplement.
**Carol Daley
Pomona Road, R D 1, Upper Moutere,
Nelson Phone/Fax (03) 540 2772**

Nuts
Macadamia Homeland Orchards
**Marjorie Clark
Phone (09) 407 9177
and**
Nut Master
**Yannick Wakelam Phone (09) 407 7417
RD2, Waipapa, Kerikeri, Bay of Islands**
Macadamia nuts, naturally grown. For eating raw as appetisers, or roasted, in salads, for cakes and ice creams. Delicious, wholesome and NATURAL.

Wines

Holmes Brothers

Richmond Plains. BIO-GRO Certified fine wines from the Nelson region. Available direct from the vineyard. Get on the mailing list to receive up-to-date tasting notes and details of special offers.
The Holmes Vineyard, McShanes Road Richmond, Nelson
Phone/Fax (03) 544 4230

The Millton Vineyard

BIO-GRO Certified. Organically grown and bottled at Millton Vineyard. Award winning and internationally acclaimed. Cited as among "best producers" of Chenin Blanc in New Zealand in the Apple international publication *Appreciating Fine Wines* by Jim Budd.
PO Box 66, Manutuke, Gisborne
Phone (06) 862 8680 Fax (06) 862 8869

Rippon Vineyard

Award winning wines organically grown and produced and BIO-GRO Certified. Visit the vineyard on Mount Aspiring Road and experience the difference.
Mount Aspiring Road, Lake Wanaka, Central Otago
Phone/Fax (03) 443 8084

MOUNT ASPIRING ROAD
LAKE WANAKA

Phone/Fax (03) 443 8084

**UNCLE TOBYS
ORGANIC WHEAT BISCUITS**
Free from artificial colours, flavours,
preservatives and chemical contaminants.
Made using only pure organic wheat
which is grown, transported and stored
without the use of artificial chemicals.

*UNCLE TOBYS ORGANIC WHEAT IS
CERTIFIED BY NASAA TO GUARANTEE IT IS TRULY ORGANIC
(NASAA — National Association for Sustainable Agriculture
Australia)*

Manufacturers and Suppliers

Biscuits
Uncle Tobys Organic Wheat Biscuits
Free from artificial colours, flavours,
preservatives and chemical contaminants.
Certified by National Association for
Sustainable Agriculture, Australia (NASAA).
**Uncle Tobys Customer Information
Phone 0800 730 123**

Bread
The Devonport Stone Oven Bakery
Makers of tasty organic Sourdough Breads 7
days a week. Also meat, vegetarian pies,
vegan muffins and other quality cakes,
pastries, slices and other specialties — made
with only the FINEST ingredients.
**The Devonport Stone Oven Bakery
12C Clarence Street
Devonport
Phone (09) 445 3185 Fax (09) 446 1065**

Frozen vegetables
Wattie Frozen Foods
Wattie Frozen Foods has a range of Organic
frozen vegetables certified by BIO-GRO.
The range includes Peas, Corn, and Mixed
Vegetables. The products are available in
selected supermarkets and Health Stores
throughout New Zealand.
**The Wattie's Good Food Centre
Phone 0800 653 050**

Meats
West Lynn Organic Meats
Specialist in Organic Meats. Preservative
free sausages, FREE RANGE CHICKENS
and EGGS. Courier service available.
**440 Richmond Road, Grey Lynn,
Auckland
Phone Brian or Hoani on (09) 376 1439**

Milk, Yoghurt and Sour Cream
Intermilk
NZ Fresh wholemilk sourced from farms
adhering to **Demeter Biodynamic Farming**
regulations and certification. Guaranteed
FREE of man-made herbicides, pesticides
and other chemicals (see advertisment on
the following page).
**P O Box 10052, Mt Maunganui
(Owens Place)
Phone 0800 656 455 for stockist details
Phone (07) 575 7003 Fax (07) 575 7250**

Serra Natural Foods
Manufactures and markets the popular
CYCLOPS brand of organic yoghurt and
organic sour cream. There are five delicious
flavours of yoghurt including Reduced Fat,
Thick N Creamy, Boysenberry, Apricot and
Walnut and Honey. These products are
available from most supermarkets.
For more information contact:
**Serra Natural Foods
PO Box 9336,
Christchurch
Phone (03) 349 6062**

WEST LYNN

ORGANIC MEATS

SPECIALIST IN

■ Organic Meats ■ Preservative-free Sausages ■ Free-range Chickens and Eggs

■ COURIER SERVICE AVAILABLE

Phone Brian or Hoani on 376 1439
440 Richmond Road ■ Grey Lynn ■ Auckland

Preserves
Phoenix Natural Foods Ltd

Hand made organic **PRESERVES** — 100% natural. Honey sweetened. Made in New Zealand from BIO-GRO Certified fruit. Also **PHOENIX NATURAL DRINKS**: Mineral Water both plain and naturally flavoured with Feijoa or Melon. Also Cola, Lemonade and Ginger Beer.

NO ARTIFICIAL FLAVOURS OR PRESERVATIVES ADDED. NATURALLY SWEETENED WITHOUT SUGAR

Call or write for the name of your nearest stockist:

Phoenix Natural Foods Ltd,
P O Box 20 217, Glen Eden, Auckland.
Phone (09) 836 2272 Fax (09) 836 5232

Free
of man-made herbicides, pesticides and chemicals.

NZ Fresh Organic Whole Milk is a full cream pasteurised milk, sourced from farms adhering to "Demeter" Biodynamic Farming regulations and certification. Demeter is an international trademark recognising organic and environmentally sustainable agriculture. Using biodynamic and natural fertilisers ensures pasture and animals grow and live under completely natural influences, and the milk is guaranteed free of man-made herbicides, pesticides and other chemicals.

Look for NZ Fresh Organic Whole Milk at your local store, or call 0800 656 455 for stockist details.

ORGANIC KITCHEN EQUIPMENT

Vitalife NZ

Champion Juicer's masticating (Juicernon-centrifugal) action produces high quality juice from vegetables and fruit. Easy to assemble and clean; robust 1/3 h.p. motor. Also grates and homogenizes for nut butters, purees, soups, frozen desserts. Optional Grain Mill attachment. Also Wheatgrass Juicers and other health appliances.

NZ Distributor:
Vitalife NZ
Peta Offa, Owhiwa Road,
R D 1, Onerahi, Northland.
Phone/Fax (09) 436 5656
Mobile (025) 812 918

If you would like to advertise in the next edition of
The Organic Kitchen
please contact:
David Bateman Ltd,
PO 100 242 NSMC
Auckland 10
Ph (09) 415 7664
Fax (09) 415 8892

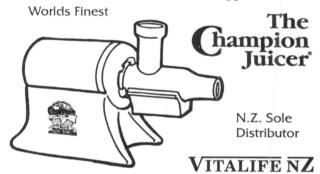